POSTCARD MEMORIES
From World War Two

Finding Lost Keepsakes 70 Years Later

By John F. Schlatter

Editorial Consultant: Sandra W. Plant
Graphics Support: Michael Wescott, Chickenhouse Graphics

Contents

It Started On A Whim

One day in 2009, mostly on a whim, I committed a random act of kindness that has paid me back many times over. It started in 2003 when I began collecting postcards written by soldiers during World War II. After several years of sporadic collecting, I decided it would be fun to track down the people who wrote the cards, or their children, and surprise them with a gift of a family memento from long ago.

Among my postcards was one from a female Marine, Private Cecilia Aragon, written in 1942 to one of her former teachers in New Mexico. I searched the internet for Private Aragon and learned that she had passed away. With a little more searching I found her daughter and sent her the card. Her daughter was grateful, and I was hooked. I knew this was something I wanted to pursue.

There was also a personal motivation. My "Greatest Generation" parents had recently passed away. After their deaths I came to treasure mementos from their lives, and I figured other Baby Boomers felt the same. I realized the World War II postcards I was finding on eBay and in antique stores were part of someone's family history, so I set out to find the soldiers, their families, and their stories. My postcard search began as a casual hobby, but the stories I uncovered were so intriguing I decided to share them in this book.

My interest in postcards began quite by accident on a summer afternoon in 2003 in Florence, Colo., a pleasant town known for the unlikely combination of antique stores and prisons, including the Federal Supermax. My wife Becky and I were lingering in a "junk store" longer than usual, trapped by a ferocious Rocky Mountain hail storm.

In those days I didn't normally look at postcards in antique stores, but out of boredom I picked up a stack of them. As I thumbed through the cards, a batch of seven cards addressed to people in Livermore Falls, Maine, piqued my interest. How did seven postcards written by soldiers in World War II to people in a small New England town show up 70 years later in an antique shop 2,000 miles away? Who were the soldiers? Who were the people they wrote to back home? What happened to them during and after the war? Are the men who wrote the cards still living? How did something so personal get away

1

from the family? Curiosity got the best of me and I spent a few dollars to buy the cards.

Over the next few years I bought more cards, but it was not until 2009 that I had the idea of returning a card to the writer or his family. After sending that first card to Cecilia Aragon's daughter I intended to continue finding soldiers or their relatives and returning the postcards. However, like many good intentions, this one didn't happen. My job got in the way and I didn't get back to the postcards until two years later. By the time I started seriously searching in 2011 the internet had evolved to the point where such sleuthing was relatively easy. My best sources were the National Archives online database of World War II enlistments, and the web sites www.ancestry.com and www.findagrave.com. (In this book I refer to them as "Ancestry" and "Findagrave.") When I found the writer or a relative I sent them the card (at no cost to them). I was rewarded with wonderful, inspiring stories of ordinary Americans called upon to do extraordinary things.

Their stories are as varied as the people who wrote the postcards.

- A sailor who served in the Pacific sent his wife in Connecticut a humorous greeting on their anniversary. The card was lost in a flood in 1955. I found his widow in Florida and returned the card to her nearly 70 years after he wrote it.
- A soldier sent a postcard to his little sister in Nebraska apologizing because he forgot to send her chewing gum. He was a chaplain's assistant in the Army and went on to become a minister. I returned the card to his little sister, now 80+ years old and a great-grandmother, and received a cordial letter from her.
- A young woman wrote to her soldier boyfriend, reminiscing about their tearful farewell in New York's Penn Station. He came home safely after the war. They were married for more than 60 years and are buried alongside each other in California, their names inscribed together on a military grave marker.
- A young pilot from Maryland wrote a postcard to his little sister, who later became an Army nurse. He was killed in the Battle of the Bulge. I returned the card to one of his relatives in Montana.

2

The family is still searching for his beautiful Welsh war bride who visited his parents in 1946 then disappeared. If she's still living she would be about 90.

- Two Army lieutenants from North Dakota became friends while attending Officer Candidate School. When the wife of one of the men gave birth to a baby boy in Kansas in 1943, the other lieutenant wrote a letter from North Africa welcoming the child to "this complex world." The letter writer went on to be a noted journalist. I found that baby boy, now a retired Los Angeles police officer, and returned the letter to him.

- A man from Pennsylvania sent a card to his future wife's family. He became a B-24 tail-gunner, was shot down over German territory and threatened with execution after being captured by the enemy. I returned his postcard to him just weeks before he passed away. His family shared with me his account of captivity and a poem titled "To My Brother In The Service," written by his 15-year-old sister during the war.

- A soldier from Michigan sent his bride a postcard full of loving thoughts. He had only a fleeting time with her before shipping off to Europe, where he was killed in action in the closing days of the war. I returned the card to his sister, who told me the family learned of his death the day before Germany surrendered. Until I sent her the postcard and information from the internet, she didn't know where her brother was buried. As it happened, the sister lives in my wife's hometown, and we had a wonderful visit with her.

- Another soldier from Michigan sent a postcard to his cousin. The card led me to the story of two brothers killed in the war, their courageous double-gold-star mother, and the nephews who bear their names.

The messages on the cards are usually routine and necessarily brief. Many begin with "Just a note to let you know . . .," and promise "I'll write a letter when I have more time." The weather and the soldier's next assignment are common topics, and there's almost always a greeting to "the folks back home." While the messages may be perfunctory, the cards tell a story of the tremendous upheaval caused by

World War II; of farm boys, college students, coal miners, store clerks, dentists and factory workers plucked from their routine lives and sent off to war.

Most of my "postcard people" survived the war, returned to their interrupted lives and, in many cases, had marriages of 60 or more years. Others never made it home. Their story ended with a white cross in a foreign cemetery, a notation on a casualty list, and perhaps their name on a marker in the family plot or a monument on the courthouse lawn.

Behind every one of these postcards I found the account of an unsung hero and his or her family. I hope you enjoy reading these stories as much as I enjoyed researching and writing them.

Cecilia Aragon, USMC

FROM: Private Cecilia Aragon; Camp Lejune, N.C; 1942

TO: Miss Alice Miller; Allison James School; Santa Fe, N.M.

MESSAGE: *"Dear Miss Miller. I am enjoying my training very much.
The country here is beautiful. Remember me to Misses Krebs and
Schwengert (?) and Mr. (illegible). Hope I may hear from you.
Sincerely, Cecilia."*

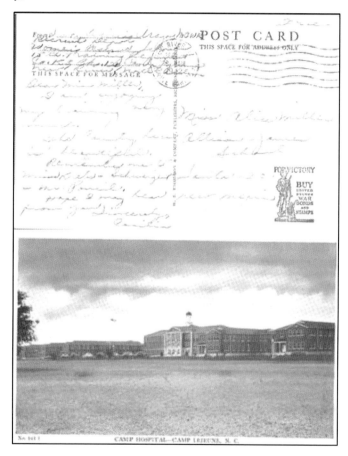

The first postcard I ever returned to a family was written by a female Marine. When I spotted the card on eBay I thought, "There must be a good story here." As it turned out, "good story" was an understatement.

In 1942, Marine Private Cecilia Aragon (who became Cecilia Guzman upon her marriage after the war) mailed a postcard from New River, N.C., to one of her former teachers at a school in Santa Fe, N.M. The card was eventually acquired by someone in Idaho who put it on eBay, and I bought it in 2008. There's no way of knowing where it was during the intervening 66 years.

A quick Google search found the obituary of Cecilia Aragon Guzman, which led me to her daughter, Dr. Nadyne Guzman, then a college professor in Colorado Springs. Coincidentally I once lived in Pueblo, Colo., not far from Colorado Springs, but moved to Kentucky shortly before finding the postcard. It's likely I passed close to Dr. Guzman's home on my frequent trips to "The Springs" as it's called in Southern Colorado.

It's usually hard to find an email address for someone, but since Dr. Guzman worked at a university it was easy to locate her. This was my first attempt to contact a relative, and I was a bit worried about what the response might be. Would she be happy to hear from me, or think I'm a scam artist? Maybe she got rid of the card in the first place and didn't want to be bothered. Maybe there's some dark family secret and I would be reopening old wounds. Regardless of my concerns, I sent an email:

"Dear Dr. Guzman:

"I collect postcards written by soldiers during World War II and recently bought one written by a Marine Corps Pvt. Cecilia Aragon in 1942. It piqued my interest because it was from a female Marine at a time when there weren't many women in the Marine Corps. It was mailed from New River, N.C,. to a Miss Alice Miller at the Allison-James School in Santa Fe, NM. Images of the front and back of the postcard are attached. I bought it from an eBay seller in Hayden, Idaho.

"My internet research indicates that Pvt. Aragon is probably your late mother. From reading her obituary in the Rocky Mountain

6

News it's obvious she was a very accomplished and caring person. The obituary listed your name, and I found your email address through the UCCS web site.

"If this card was indeed written by your mother and you want it, I'll be happy to send it to you at no cost. Having lost my own mother a couple of years ago I know how important such mementos can be.

"Best regards,

"John Schlatter"

Much to my relief and delight, she sent me the following gracious reply:

"Mr. Schlatter,

"I am so touched by your generosity! Yes, the postcard was from my mother to a former teacher at Allison James in Santa Fe. That school no longer exists, but the high school in Albuquerque she attended, Menaul School, is still in operation. The events that brought my mother to attend boarding school are many and my grandfather worked three jobs to pay for her tuition.

"My mother was a risk taker in her young adult years, but took the risks because she learned from her father, a WWI veteran, "for God and country." She worked for the Army Corps of Engineers during the first part of the war and was invited to work in Los Alamos. She chose to enter the Marine Corps, instead, and worked as a payroll clerk in Washington, DC where she met the men memorialized in the Iwo Jima memorial.

"I was fortunate to have my parents living with me for the last seven years of their lives. My dad, a veteran of the Army Air Corps, died in May 2008 and my mother missed him greatly. She declared she was ready to join "Gus and God" the day after her 88th birthday, came home from the hospital and passed away three days later. One of her friends from her Marine days still lives in Florida.

"Yes, please send me the postcard as I will be so pleased to have it. I still have her Marine cap—and one from the Marine Corps League she joined several years ago.

"You are so kind to reach out to me. May God's blessings of love and joy and peace and grace be with you.

7

"Nadyne Guzman"

So my first attempt to "reunite" a card with the family of its author was a success. I was delighted to make the connection and to learn about Private Aragon. I learned more about this remarkable woman from her obituary:

"She was born Oct. 2, 1920, in Alamosa to Manuel Aragón and Juanita (Suazo) Aragón, Cecilia was the only one of four siblings to survive childhood. She graduated from Menaul High School, a Presbyterian boarding school in Albuquerque, NM. After a short time attending the University of New Mexico, she went on to study at a private business college and then took a job in Santa Fe, NM, with the Army Corps of Engineers. During World War II, Cece proudly joined the United States Marine Corps as one of the first women to be inducted into the Corps. After the war, she moved to San Bernardino, Calif. to serve as a Presbyterian missionary where she met and married Guadalupe Guzmán."

Cecilia and Guadalupe "Gus" Guzman married in 1946. He was also a veteran, having served in the Army Air Corps in Egypt, Libya, Tunisia, Italy, France, Germany, and England. They settled in her hometown of Alamosa in Colorado's beautiful San Luis Valley and became mainstays of the community. In addition to her career at a savings and loan, Cecilia was a leader in her church and a founding board member of La Puente, a non-profit that provides shelter and assistance for homeless individuals and families. Gus was also active in church and community.

Cecilia Aragon Guzman exemplifies the countless World War II veterans who served their country, then went back home to raise a family and help others.

I Celebrated Our Anniversary With A Shot – Of Typhoid

FROM: Gustave Luschenat; U.S. Navy Training Center; Sampson, N.Y.; August 8, 1944

TO: His wife Josephine Luschenat in Waterbury, Conn.

MESSAGE: *"Dear Hon, I celebrated our anniversary with a shot – of typhoid. Love, Gus."*

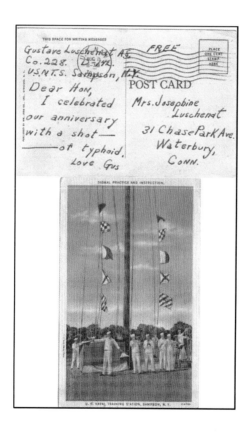

If I have a favorite postcard, this is it.

Gus Luschenat's humorous anniversary postcard to his wife Josephine reached her twice -- once in 1944 in Connecticut, and again in Florida 68 years later. During those years the card sat in a house in Connecticut, was lost in a flood, reappeared in an antique store in Colorado, and traveled with me to Kentucky and Maryland before finding its way back to Josephine in Florida.

Gustave James Luschenat enlisted in the Navy July 14, 1944. When he wrote to Josephine back home in Waterbury, Conn., three weeks later, his brief note spoke volumes about the plight of young couples during World War II. Postmarked August 8, 1944 from a Navy boot camp at Sampson, N.Y., the card simply said:

> *"Dear Hon:*
> *"I celebrated our anniversary with a shot --- of typhoid.*
> *"Love, Gus."*

Were it not for the war, Gus and Josephine would have celebrated that anniversary together. Instead, she was living with her parents and he was at boot camp, wondering where the Navy would send him next.

When I saw the card in an antique store in Colorado in 2003 I had to have it. I was struck by the ability of this young man to make a joke about getting a typhoid shot instead of having "a shot" with his wife on their anniversary. I made a few fruitless efforts to find Gus and Josephine online in 2003, and then put the card away. It sat in a cigar box with other cards as I moved first to Kentucky then to Maryland. In early 2012 I tried again to locate them.

Gus Luschenat

I learned that Gus died in 1990 and found an address for Josephine, who was living in Florida. My letter to her was quickly answered with a lovely handwritten note on flowered stationery. I had often wondered why a postcard with such obvious sentimental value was no longer with the family. Josephine's letter explained it all:

"Dear John and Becky:

"I was pleasantly surprised to get your letter today. As I have been home, sick in bed, this brightened my day.

"In August 1955 we had a devastating flood in Waterbury, Conn. Many died and my father's home was condemned. We were sent to a girls' school in Middlebury, Conn., until we were able to rent another place. I'm sure mementos of my husband were lost at that time.

"My husband went on to the South Pacific during World War II, stationed in the Marshall Islands on a crash boat."

Military records on Ancestry list Gus on the "muster roll" of Aviation Rescue Boat C-21001 at the Russell Islands in July 1945. As the name implies, Aviation Rescue Boats were deployed to rescue downed pilots. The Russell Islands were used by the Navy as a staging area. John F. Kennedy's PT-109 was berthed there briefly in June 1944, two months before its fateful encounter with a Japanese destroyer.

Gus went back to Connecticut after the war, where he was a tool maker and Josephine worked in the records department of a hospital. They moved to Florida in retirement.

Like many of my "postcard people," the Luschenat family continued a military tradition. Gus and Josephine had a son who served with distinction as an Air Force pilot, retiring as a Lieutenant Colonel.

As soon as I knew I had a good address for Josephine I sent her the postcard. Receiving her letter was one of the most touching experiences of my postcard searches. As I read Josephine's letter aloud to my wife Becky, there wasn't a dry eye in our apartment when I got to the part where she spoke of Gus:

"He died 20 years ago. I miss him still."

I Am That Little Sister, 70 Years Later

FROM: Sergeant August Mommens, Columbus, Miss.; November 1943

TO: His little sister Vernabelle Mommens; Tecumseh, Nebraska

MESSAGE: *"Hey, it looks like I kind of let you down on the gum I was going to send. Well, I'll get it sent tomorrow I hope. Am fine. Be good and write."*

     A soldier's promise to send chewing gum to his little sister led me to a remarkable man from Nebraska and to the little sister, now a great-grandmother with fond girlhood memories of her big brother.

     In early 2012 I found a postcard on eBay with the following message:

     "It looks like I kind of let you down on the gum I was going to send. Well, I'll get it sent tomorrow I hope. Am fine. Be good and write."

     The author was Sgt. August Mommens, an Army chaplain's assistant, writing from Mississippi to his little sister Vernabelle back home in Tecumseh, Neb., in November 1943. Nearly 70 years later his card had somehow made its way to an eBay seller in Pennsylvania. "Mommens" is not a common name, so it didn't take long for me to find the card's author through an obituary published in 2005.

"The Reverend August W. Mommens, pastor emeritus, St. Libory, Nebraska, departed this life on Tuesday, September 20, 2005, at the age of 87. He was born at Tecumseh, Nebraska, on October 22, 1917, to William C. and Kathrine (Albers) Mommens. Pastor Mommens worked with the Civilian Conservation Corps until entering the U.S. Army Air Corps in February, 1941. He served as a Chaplain's Assistant and was discharged in November, 1945. He married Loraine Stichweh on June 2, 1946, at Plymouth. He graduated from Concordia Theological Seminary, Springfield, Illinois, in 1952 and served congregations in Iowa, Nebraska, North Dakota, Florida, and Oregon. He also served as Chaplain at the Nebraska Veterans Home in Grand Island from 1972-1982. Following his retirement from the Veterans Home, he worked with Laborers for Christ for ten years."

Reading between the lines, and learning about the family from census records, I began to understand the work ethic that must have been the hallmark of August Mommens' life. As the third of seven children (and the eldest son) in a Nebraska farm family, he surely had plenty of responsibilities growing up. Being the ripe old age of 23 when he enlisted in 1941, he was older than most of the 18- and 19-year-old recruits swelling the ranks of the Army. The youngsters probably looked up to him as an old man. And notwithstanding the financial help of the GI bill, it must have taken great dedication and perseverance for him to earn a theological degree at the age of 35, more than six years after he left the Army and got married.

As noted in the obituary, Rev. Mommens served numerous congregations in five states. But his service to his church didn't stop there. After he retired from the ministry at age 65, he spent another 10 years helping build church buildings through the Lutheran organization Laborers for Christ.

Survivors listed in Rev. Mommens' obituary included his wife, 11 children, 37 grandchildren, 29 great-grandchildren, and one great-great-grandchild. Oh yes – and his sister Vernabelle, the one he promised chewing gum in 1943. I couldn't find an address for

Vernabelle, but I did find Rev. Mommens' son, David. When I sent him an email asking if the family would like to have the postcard, he replied:

"God's blessings to you. I would very much appreciate acquiring the post card. I would be happy to cover any expense you might have in sending it to me. My aunt would be overjoyed to see it and have it as a remembrance of my father."

Like his late father, David Mommens is a minister. When I tracked him down on the internet I found a photo of a distinguished silver-haired man in a clerical collar gently cradling a baby in his arms. I suspect the apple didn't fall far from the tree.

This particular card traveled from Sgt. Mommens in Mississippi, to his sister in Nebraska, to an eBay seller in Pennsylvania, to me in Maryland, to David Mommens in Indiana, and finally, after 69 years, back to Vernabelle in Nebraska.

I had solved the mystery of the postcard, but there was still one unanswered question. Did Vernabelle ever get her chewing gum? The answer came in a thank-you card and hand-written note from Vernabelle Mommens Adams. She wrote:

"A few weeks back you corresponded with a Rev. David Mommens regarding a postcard written by August Mommens, a soldier in the Army during WWII in November of 1943. He promised to send his little sister some gum.

"I am that little sister – 70 years later, 80+ years old, grandmother and great grandma too. And strangely enough, I don't

remember ever getting any gum. I received other things, but I can't remember gum. Maybe it followed the card.

"Anyway, what a great and wonderful thing to do. Your care, concern and generosity is deeply appreciated. "Thank you" is so little to say for such a good deed.

"My family certainly enjoyed it as will others in the future.

"Good luck, Vernabelle"

I'll Never Forget The Feeling Of Seeing That American Flag

FROM: PFC Clark McWilliams; Ft. Lewis, Wash.; Dec. 8, 1943.

TO: Mr. and Mrs. Ferree; Jacobus, Penn. (In 1947 he married their daughter Virginia, who is mentioned in the card.

MESSAGE: *"Hello folks. Well, I am now on my way to the Air Corps. I am detached from the 44th. Don't write to my above address. Wait until I get settled at my Air Corps base. How is Gin? Tell her I said hello and all my love. Mac."*

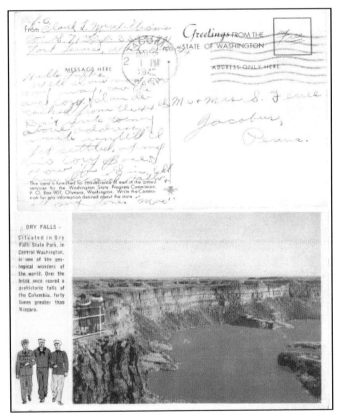

Of the twenty or so soldiers whose postcards I reconnected, only a few were still living when I searched for them. One of them was Clark

McWilliams of York, Penn., whose card I returned just three weeks before he died on April 24, 2012, at age 89. I hope that in some small way the postcard brought a smile to his face during his final days. His daughter shared her dad's story with me, and what a story it is!

My search for Clark McWilliams started when I acquired through eBay a postcard he wrote to his future in-laws in Jacobus, Penn., in December 1943. Mailed from Ft. Lewis, Wash., the card said he was now in the Air Corps and would send them his new address as soon as he had it.

This card caught my attention for several reasons, including attributes that made it easier to track. The name of the sender was clearly legible, the soldier didn't have a common name, and the card was mailed to a small town.

Additionally, I recognized the scene on the front of the card. During World War II, the State of Washington provided free postcards to soldiers as a way of promoting their state. This particular card pictured Dry Falls, a place I visited several times while living in Richland, Wash., in the mid 1990s.

Finding Clark McWilliams or his family was not as easy as I had hoped. After several dead ends I found a message his daughter, Joni McKenzie, posted on a genealogy web site in 2006. That message included an email address, but when I emailed her the address was no longer valid. After more searching I found her new email address on a presentation she made in her job at a school district. I sent a note and she wrote back:

"Thank you so much for contacting me! Yes, Clark McWilliams is my father and Mr. and Mrs. Ferree are my grandparents. We would love to have the postcard. I have been compiling dad's correspondence, documents and photos from WWII. We will add it to our cherished collection.

"Your timing is a real godsend. My dad is not doing well, and this will bring a smile to his face.

"Thank you very much for your kind and thoughtful act!"

I sent her the postcard right away. A few weeks later she wrote back:

"Thank you so much for sending us the postcard. It was wonderful to share it with our family over the holiday break. And Dad enjoyed the story.

"Our father will not be with us for much longer. He is the last surviving member of his B24 crew. Only 2 survived when their plane was shot down. We have attached a few things that we have tried to record. (Also a poem that was written by his sister, Aunita, and a picture of Dad and Aunita.) Dad did not really talk about his WWII experience until 1985. That year he attended an army reunion with the men that he went through basic training with. When he came back from that reunion, he talked more about his experience -- if you would ask him.*

Clark McWilliams

"With Dad's passing, there will be no one left to tell their story -- no one but us. I hope you enjoy his story.

"Again, thank you for sending us the postcard."

In the course of our email exchange, Joni sent me her father's written account of his wartime experience. He began by telling how he joined the Army:

"After hearing the news of Pearl Harbor, a group of guys from Glen Rock went up to Harrisburg to enlist in the Army. I believe there were 10 of us. On the way back, nine had joined the army. The only one left out was me; I didn't make it in at the time because I was too skinny!

"Eventually, I received my draft notice – then I was good enough! On February 23, 1943, I enlisted in the Army."

He told how, after receiving training in the U.S., he was stationed in Foggia, Italy, as part of a B-24 crew:

Clark McWilliams (first row, far right) with his B-24 flight crew comrades in Italy.

"From Foggia, we flew twelve combat missions. Our mission was usually to fly and bomb Gratz, Austria. For these missions we did not fly the same plane. We flew whatever was on the ground and available. On our 12th mission we were shot down by German anti-aircraft guns over Austria. The date was March 23, 1945. The front of the airplane was hit hard. Five people in the front of the plane were killed: 1st Lt. James L. Thomas, pilot; Lt. Frank K. Lee, Flight Officer, Lt. Peter P. Mahoney, Jr., Flight Officer and Bombardier, Staff Sergeant William C. McDonald, Nose Gunner, Sergeant Lowell "Whitey" Nyborg, Top Gunner. Richard (Dick) Ward and I parachuted out. I was the tail gunner and Dick was the belly gunner. I lost my boots as we jumped! (I later found out that on April 6, 1945, my 22nd birthday, my mother and father received a letter from the army notifying them that I was missing in action.)"

He went on to describe parachuting from the downed plane, landing in a tree, and being captured. One of his captors kicked him in the mouth, breaking his two front teeth. His description of his first night in captivity is a masterpiece of understatement:

"They told us they would put us in a room and execute us in the morning. Needless to say it was a long night."

19

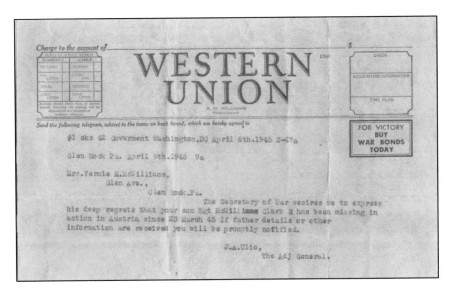

Charge to the account of_____ $_____

WESTERN UNION

A. N. WILLIAMS
PRESIDENT

FOR VICTORY
BUY
WAR BONDS
TODAY

Send the following telegram, subject to the terms on back hereof, which are hereby agreed to

#1 cks 42 Govrrment Washington,DC April 6th.1945 2-47a

Glen Rock Pa. April 6th.1945 9a

Mrs.Vernie M.McWilliams,
Glen Ave.,
Glen Rock,Pa.

The Secretary of War desires me to express his deep regrets that your son Sgt McWilliams Clark R has been missing in action in Austria since 23 March 45 If futher details or other information are received you will be promptly notified.

J.A.Ulio,
The Adj General.

Clark McWilliams' parents received this telegram notifying them their son was missing in action. The telegram is dated April 6, 1945, his 22nd birthday.

He wasn't executed. Instead of being shot he was sent to a prison camp.

"We were asked if we wanted to walk or take the train. We decided to walk because our forces were strafing (shooting) the trains because they may have been carrying German troops. I was given boots to replace the ones I had lost. My feet blistered due to the poor shoes. On our first day of marching, we were strafed by our own planes by mistake. We made signs with our clothing saying POW. We were marching to Nuremburg Interrogation Center. I believe we were on the road for about thirty days. I remember our bombers dropped leaflets letting us know the end was coming soon.

"We never made it to Nuremburg. One day, we spotted the American flag coming up over the top of a hill. And behind the flag came our troops. I'll never forget the feeling of seeing that American flag as it crested the hill."

Joni also sent me a poem written by Clark's sister Aunita, who survives him. She wrote the poem when she was 15 while he was stationed at Ft. Lewis, the place from which he wrote the postcard. The poem is titled, "To My Brother in the Service." The poem is reproduced on a following page, along with a photo of Aunita and Clark together during the war. Her poem captured the emotions millions of families

20

must have felt toward their brothers, sons, husbands, and boyfriends in the service.

One line of the poem says, "God bless our boy in the service, watch over him both night and day, and when this war is over, please send him home we pray." Aunita's prayer was answered. Her brother returned home to a happy marriage of 65 years, a career with the local school district, and 25 years of public service. Clark McWilliams died April 24, 2012, survived by his wife, Virginia, along with numerous children, grandchildren, and one great-grandchild. In addition to his family, his legacy includes a 40-year career with the York Suburban Area School District and 25 years of community service as a member of the Jacobus Borough Council.

Clark McWilliams and his sister Aunita. At age 15 she wrote a poem "To My Brother In The Service."

There are many heroic and exciting things Clark McWilliams could have said about himself, but like most of his World War II comrades he was not one to brag. He concluded the account of his wartime experience with the simple joy of coming home:

"We were taken to LeHarve, France, by train and truck. Then we were shipped home. Before I was discharged I went to Tyndale Air Force Base, Florida, to have my front teeth fixed. I received my honorable discharge on November 30, 1945. I was discharged from Middleton Air Force Base. I made it home to Glen Rock!"

To My Brother In The Service

When Clark McWilliams was serving in the Army his sister Aunita, then 15, wrote this poem. His daughter, Joni McKenzie, provided a copy of the poem and a photo of Aunita and Clark during the war.

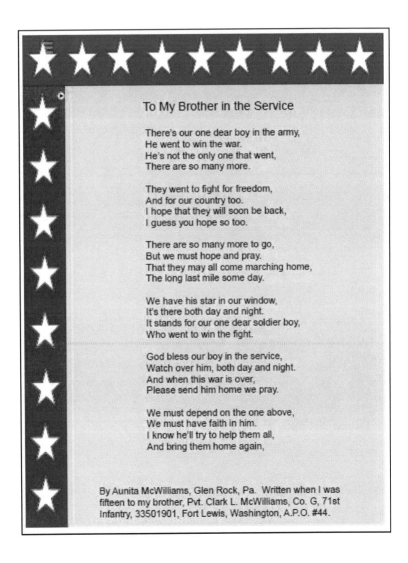

To My Brother in the Service

There's our one dear boy in the army,
He went to win the war.
He's not the only one that went,
There are so many more.

They went to fight for freedom,
And for our country too.
I hope that they will soon be back,
I guess you hope so too.

There are so many more to go,
But we must hope and pray.
That they may all come marching home,
The long last mile some day.

We have his star in our window,
It's there both day and night.
It stands for our one dear soldier boy,
Who went to win the fight.

God bless our boy in the service,
Watch over him, both day and night.
And when this war is over,
Please send him home we pray.

We must depend on the one above,
We must have faith in him.
I know he'll try to help them all,
And bring them home again,

By Aunita McWilliams, Glen Rock, Pa. Written when I was fifteen to my brother, Pvt. Clark L. McWilliams, Co. G, 71st Infantry, 33501901, Fort Lewis, Washington, A.P.O. #44.

Didn't Get Any Mail From You Today

FROM: PFC Fred Hegler; Wichita Falls, Texas; Oct. 22, 1945

TO: His mother in Pueblo, Colo.

MESSAGE: *"Mom and All: I got the new suit and it is really not bad, but I thought it would be better, it was better than the one Gordon sent. Well I am fine – didn't get any mail from you today."*

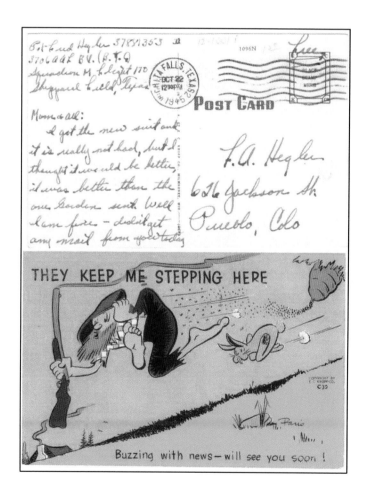

For many young men the first weeks of Army life were lonely times, hoping every day for a letter or a package from the folks back home. It's understandable that a soldier might sometimes feel sorry for himself. That was apparently the case with Fred Hegler when he wrote the following to his parents in October 1945, one month into his basic training in Texas:

"Mom and All:

"I got the new suit and it is really not bad, but I thought it would be better, it was better than the one Gordon sent. Well I am fine – didn't get any mail from you today."

Fred was from Pueblo, Colo. I lived there in 2003-2007 and bought this card in an antique store near Pueblo around 2003. I didn't try to locate Fred until several years later. Given the fact that the card was written by a local person, I assumed the family had put it up for sale and didn't want it.

By the time I started tracking down postcard writers in 2011 I had left Pueblo. I found that Fred was still living and quite active into his eighties. I also found that Fred and I were more connected than I realized.

When I lived in Pueblo, I worked at an office near the historic Union Depot. Every day on the way to work I passed a store called "Fred's Paints." The sign on the store featured a distinctive figure of a man holding out a paintbrush and lifting his knee so his body formed the letter "F" in the word "Fred's." While living in Pueblo I created a poster called the "Pueblo Alphabet." It featured all 26 letters of the alphabet from landmarks around town, and I used the Fred's Paints sign for the letter "F."

It turned out that Fred Hegler founded Fred's Paints and still goes to the office several days a week. I wrote to Fred asking if he wanted the postcard, and enclosed a small image of the Pueblo Alphabet poster. In reply I got a very nice email from his wife, Betty, writing on Fred's behalf as his eyesight was failing. She said they liked the card, but they liked the poster even more and were using a magnifying glass to identify the letters. She said Fred has a box full of his postcards and other correspondence from the war, adding that they are puzzled as to how this one card ended up in an antique store.

I sent them the postcard, along with a full-sized poster of the Pueblo Alphabet. I hope Fred liked the poster more than he liked the suit he received back in 1945.

I Would Like For You To Write Me A Few Letters

FROM: Private Sid Campbell; Alexandria, La.; March 3, 1943

TO: A girl named Sue in Metairie, La. (I'm not using Sue's last name, as I was unable to locate her or her family).

MESSAGE: *"Dear Sue. Sorry for not writing sooner but my work keeps me plenty busy. Right now it's 19 degrees and I'm freezing. As soon as I get shipped to my permanent station I'll write. Give your folks my regards. Sidney"*

(The cartoon on Sid's card says, "The Army only has two sizes, too small and too big." The same card was sent by Private Francis Folsom, whose story is told in a later chapter.)

FROM: Private David Henson; Camp Butner, N.C.; May 20, 1943

TO: That same girl named Sue in Metairie, La.

MESSAGE: *"Hello Sue. Will write to let you hear from me. I got your address from Sid Campbell. He's a good guy. I would like for you to write me a few letters if you can. It would make me feel good to write to a girl out there. I am from West Virginia."*

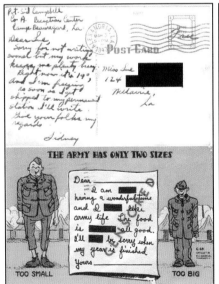

This is the story of how two postcards led me to uncover a wartime friendship that lasted for decades and return treasured mementos to two families.

In the spring of 1943 a girl named Sue in Metairie, La., received postcards from two young soldiers. One was from Sid Campbell, the other from David Henson. It's likely the cards stayed in a box at Sue's house for decades and were eventually sold at a garage or estate sale. The cards ended up in the hands of a dealer in New Jersey who put them up for sale on eBay in 2012. Intrigued by two cards from different men addressed to the same girl, I bought them.

My initial research showed that Sid was from the New Orleans area, while David was from West Virginia. Reading between the lines, it appeared Sid and Sue were friends before the war, and Sid introduced Sue to David. I jumped to the erroneous conclusion that Sid made the introductions in Louisiana, maybe at a USO dance. I conjured up an image of a wartime romance between a West Virginia boy and a Cajun queen leading to marriage, children, and a house with a white picket fence. When I studied the postmarks I realized David probably never met Sue; rather, this was the usual "soldier looking for a pen pal" story.

I've come across several World War II cards and letters in which a soldier wrote to a girl asking her to be a pen pal. In many cases he didn't know the girl and got her name from one of his Army buddies. Such was the case with these postcards to Sue. David was looking for a pen pal, and Sid suggested his friend Sue.

David Wesley Henson was from Dawes, W. Va., a tiny town along Cabin Creek Road, about 20 miles from the state capital of Charleston. Sidney W. Campbell, Jr. was a Louisiana native from near New Orleans.

Sid was born in 1924 and joined the Army in February 1943. According to his enlistment record he was a high school graduate and he was "single with no dependents." He was first sent to the Camp Beauregard Reception Center near Pineville, La., about 200 miles northwest of New Orleans. A few weeks after arriving he jotted a postcard to Sue.

Sid's card to Sue is postmarked March 3, 1943. He apparently wasn't too happy with the weather in northern Louisiana, as he wrote, *"It's 19 degrees and I'm freezing."* He also promised to write "after I get shipped to my permanent station," and closed with, "give your folks my regards."

Two months later Sue received a card postmarked May 20, 1943. This one was from David Henson, writing from Camp Butner near Durham, N.C. The card said:

"Hello Sue. Will write to let you hear from me. I got your address from Sid Campbell. He's a good guy. I would like for you to write me a few letters if you can. It would make me feel good to write to a girl out there. I am from West Virginia."

The message portion of David's card to Sue is in his own handwriting, but Sue's address and David's return address look like they were written by Sid. I found that curious, but it was explained when I started searching for Sid and David and found their enlistment records on the National Archives web site. David was a coal miner, and he was probably not a frequent letter writer. He had little formal education, and his penmanship left something to be desired. As I later learned, he dropped out of school at age 12. Sid, on the other hand, was listed as a "file clerk," a man accustomed to writing, and he had excellent penmanship. It appears Sid not only gave Sue's name to David, but also addressed the card for him.

My search for David and Sid was facilitated by their family members and the internet. David's daughter posted messages about him on genealogy web sites, and Sid's daughter-in-law wrote a note honoring him on her blog site on Veterans' Day 2009. With that information I was quickly able to locate the families of both men and return the cards to them.

I learned that Sid returned to the New Orleans area after the war and built several successful family-owned businesses. Through his daughter-in-law I was able to return his card to the family. Sid was still living when I contacted them in April 2012.

David went back to West Virginia, where he died in 2008. I located his daughter, Fran Critchfield, in Zanesville, Ohio. I sent Fran his postcard and learned her father's inspiring life story. I also learned that the two men remained friends long after the war.

Sid Campbell's son, Grant, patiently relayed my questions to his dad, who had suffered a stroke. Grant helped me piece together the story of Sid and David, their military service and post-war friendship. Sid was drafted in 1943 at the age of 18. He trained at Camp Butner in North Carolina and Camp Campbell in Kentucky. He was in combat in Europe for 10 months with the 78th Infantry Division and the 20th Armored Division. Sid was among the American troops who liberated the Dachau concentration camp on April 24, 1945.

Sid met his wife several years after the war while she was in nursing school in New Orleans. Grant related that his father was among the millions of men discharged after the war and jobs were hard to find. Sid went into business with his father in what Grant describes as a "very small roofing company." At one time that company was the largest roofing contractor in New Orleans and was entrusted to re-roof the famed St. Louis Cathedral on Jackson Square in the French Quarter. Sid later started several other successful businesses.

Sid met David Henson in 1943 at Camp Butner, and they served together in Europe. They remained friends after the war, seeing each other at reunions.

On Sept. 24, 2012, as I was preparing to publish this book, Grant let me know Sid had passed away.

David Henson

David Henson didn't have an easy life. When he was a small child in West Virginia his father took off for Kentucky, leaving David's mother alone with six children, the first of whom was born when she was 16. David had to quit school and work in the coal mines to help support the family.

From David's enlistment records I learned that when he joined the Army on March 11, 1943, just shy of his 18th birthday, the Army recorded him as "Single, With Dependents." I found it hard to grasp the concept of a 17-year-old being "Single, With Dependents."

David's enlistment record shows his occupation as "Code 922, unskilled occupations in extraction of minerals." I guess that's government-speak for "coal miner." People familiar with coal mining know the work is anything but "unskilled," and it's hard and exceedingly dangerous.

David's Army record raised a mystery. It said he was born in 1923, yet numerous other sources said he was born in 1925. Fran solved that one for me. She told me she learned from relatives that David fudged his birth date to join the Army.

When David returned to post-war West Virginia he worked 35 years for Bethlehem Mining Corporation. He married shortly after the war and his daughter Fran was born. His wife died in 1962, and he later remarried to Mary Smith Browning. They both passed away in 2008.

When Fran writes about her father, two things come through: his strong work ethic and his devotion to family. She recounts how, before he married Mary, he often worked seven days a week, 10- to 12-hour shifts. "He was truly a workaholic," Fran recalls, "never went on a vacation till they got married. That's when we all started going to Florida every June on the last day of school."

The work ethic that sent David into the coal mines at age 12 apparently stayed with him all his life. Fran writes:

"Dad was the kind who NEVER missed work. He would work all shifts then come home and work around the house. When they retired and moved to Florida they both went back to work doing something. Dad put in swimming pools, Mom went to work at a hospital. After 15 years in Florida they moved back to West Virginia. Dad went to work at a funeral home, the very one where his funeral was held. He had to be busy. To the day he collapsed he was at work planting flowers all around the funeral home. He was also a Mason and part of the UMW. He would do anything for anyone. I think the reason he felt he needed to work all the time was plainly due to hardships as a young person."

Grant Campbell told me a story he heard from his dad, Sid, about David Henson's coal mining background:

"My dad told me that during basic training everyone in their unit suffered during the long marches with 65 pound packs, but Mr. Henson thought it was nice to be outside, almost a picnic, after the grueling life in a coal mine."

David saw combat in Europe with the 78th Infantry Division. As noted on the Division's web site, the 78th fought across Belgium, France and Germany. They crossed the famed Remagen Bridgehead on the way to Berlin. Fran Critchfield says her husband researched the 78th and determined that Sid and David probably crossed the bridge within an hour of each other. After six months of occupation duty the 78th was officially deactivated in May of 1946.

Like many World War II vets, David seldom talked about his wartime experience. As Fran tells it:

"A friend of his from the war that he kept in touch with wanted to write a book about the war. He wanted Dad to tell it like it was. Dad refused by saying, 'I can't do that. I have three daughters and the world couldn't accept what REALLY happened,' so it must have been bad."

Fran sent me the link to a web site she created honoring her Dad and Mary. The photos of David show him at several points in life: a young man in his Army uniform; a handsome, middle-aged father; a proud grandfather; and, finally, a devoted, silver-haired husband, lovingly taking care of Mary as she slipped into the haze of Alzheimer's.

David Henson with his wife Mary.

David and Mary died within six months of each other in 2008. Fran's web site honoring their memory includes a photo labeled "Together Forever." It shows a brass military grave marker inscribed with their names, festooned with flowers and, fittingly, topped with an American flag.

As You Begin Life In This Complex World

FROM: Lt. George Moses; somewhere in North Africa; Sept. 9, 1943

TO: Gary Rogness, newborn son of Lt. Don Rogness, Ft. Leavenworth, Kan.

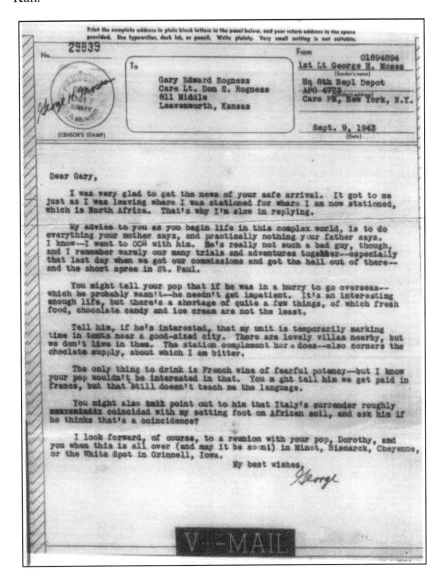

Two young men from North Dakota crossed paths for 12 weeks during Officer Candidate School (OCS) in 1942, and then went their separate ways. It's unclear if they ever met again, but they remain connected to each other, and to a retired Los Angeles police officer, by a "V-Mail" letter that was tucked away for nearly 70 years.

George Moses and Donald Rogness were both born in Minot, N.D., George in 1915 and Donald in 1920. They likely didn't know each other while growing up, as George's family moved to Bismarck when he was a child. The war brought them together in 1942 when they attended OCS at Grinnell College in Iowa.

The Army conducted wartime OCS on several college campuses throughout the country. Grinnell was home to OCS for the Adjutant General Corps, the Army's administrative officers (not to be confused with the lawyers in the Judge Advocate General Corps).

Maybe it was their shared North Dakota roots, or maybe they just hit it off, but the two men became friends during OCS. While off duty they apparently hung out at the White Spot, a popular café in Grinnell. After they were commissioned as Second Lieutenants, George was posted to North Africa and Donald to Ft. Leavenworth, Kan.

They must have stayed in touch, for when Donald's wife gave birth to a son, Gary Rogness, in 1943, George sent a letter addressed to the newborn baby in care of his father. The letter begins:

"Dear Gary: I was very glad to get the news of your safe arrival. It got to me just as I was leaving where I was stationed for where I am now stationed, which is North Africa. That's why I'm slow in replying. My advice to you as you begin life in this complex world is to do everything your mother says, and practically nothing your father says. I know – I went to OCS with him. He's really not such a bad guy, though, and I remember warmly our many trials and adventures together – especially that last day when we got our commissions and got the hell out of there – and the short spree in St. Paul."

The letter is in a five-inch by four-inch envelope marked "War & Navy Departments, V-Mail Service, Official Business." V-Mail, as I learned from the National Postal Museum, was a system originated by the British in which letters were microfilmed overseas, flown back to the States, and reprinted for delivery. This saved a huge amount of space and weight on military transports.

It's not clear where the letter languished for 69 years until I saw it listed for auction by an eBay seller in Cheyenne, Wyo., in early 2012. Although I was looking for postcards, I couldn't pass up this unique letter.

While many things about the letter intrigued me, I was particularly impressed by the writing style. With degrees in journalism and 35 years in corporate communications and newspaper work, I know good writing when I see it. As I read the letter I thought, "This guy is a good writer." As it turned out, he was more than just a good writer; he was a renowned journalist.

The letter writer, George Moses, was a reporter before the war, first for the *Bismarck Tribune* and later for the Associated Press. After the war he went back to the AP and rose to Bureau Chief in Minneapolis before retiring from AP in 1970. He then taught journalism at Macalester College in St. Paul for 10 years.

A collection of his correspondence, articles, and other papers is housed at the Minnesota Historical Society. A note to the collection says, "Though not a war correspondent, Moses wrote scores of letters and took photographs detailing his World War II experiences as a lieutenant in the U.S. Army."

George was a very witty guy. Examples can be found in two passages where he sardonically implied he was responsible for monumental events. In his 1943 letter to newborn Gary Rogness he wrote:

"You might also point out to (your father) that Italy's surrender roughly coincided with my setting foot on African soil, and ask him if he thinks that's coincidence."

Years later he penned his own obituary (a common practice among reporters and a frequent assignment in journalism school). In it he wrote:

"From 1937 to 1940 Moses was a reporter and editor on the Bismarck Tribune. (By coincidence, the Tribune won a Pulitzer Prize shortly after he joined it.)"

George died in 2007, but his legacy lives on. When he retired from Macalester College in 1980 the Minnesota Associated Press established the George Moses Award, given annually to the AP reporter deemed to have written the best story of the year.

While George returned to his journalism career after the war, his Army pal Donald Rogness moved to Cheyenne, Wyo., where he had met his wife while stationed at Fort Warren (now Warren Air Force Base). He worked for his father-in-law as a house painter and later moved to Laramie for several years before moving to California and settling in the San Fernando Valley area of Los Angeles in 1954. He and his wife divorced in 1962. He retired as the paint foreman for CBS Television Studios in 1982. Donald Rogness died in 2009 at age 89 after what his son describes as "a long and full life."

The one surviving link between these two wartime buddies is that small, yellowing letter written to Gary Rogness when he was born in 1943. I tracked Gary down and learned he's a retired Los Angeles police officer living in California. When I wrote Gary I included a line I put in most of my letters explaining my postcard hobby: "I enjoy the detective work, and it keeps me off the street." Gary replied:

"What a surprise it was to open your letter and find a copy of a letter addressed to me in care of my father dated September 9, 1943. I really got a kick out of it. That was a very kind and thoughtful thing for you to do. I didn't know the letter writer but I think I recall my dad mentioning his name years ago. Your detective skills are admirable and I say that as a retired 28-year veteran of the Los Angeles Police Department. Thanks for taking the time and effort to contact me!"

My interaction with Gary Rogness led him to an interesting discovery. I asked him for a photo of his father. When he sent the photo, he wrote:

"I've also included a note on the back of the picture that I would never have seen had it not been for your contact with me regarding your project (I had to remove the picture for scanning and discovered my dad's handwritten note to his mother (grandma Rogness) which I, in all likelihood would have never seen). So thanks again for that!"

The photo was of Lt. Donald Rogness in uniform, looking like a battle-hardened soldier. The note said:

"I'm the fellow who used to wet his diapers. Remember? I love you Mom. Your son, Don."

The whereabouts over the years of that 1943 letter from Lt. George Moses to newborn Gary Rogness remains a mystery. Gary speculates it spent most of the past six decades at his grandmother's house in Cheyenne and was eventually put in an auction or estate sale.

Like many wartime messages, the letter welcoming Gary Rogness to "this complex world" spoke of hope for better days to come. Lt. Moses wrote:

"I look forward, of course, to a reunion with your pop, Dorothy, and you when this is all over (and may it be soon!) in Minot, Bismarck, Cheyenne, or the White Spot in Grinnell, Iowa."

The White Spot is gone. The baby boy whose birth prompted the letter is retired. George Moses and Donald Rogness have passed away. I hope they really did have that reunion.

Lt. Don Rogness sent his mother this photo of himself, with a note on the back.

A Very Humble Person Who Made An Impression On Me

FROM: PFC William Halfen; Bergstrom Field, Tex.; Mar. 19, 1944

TO: His uncle, Oswald Bartsch; Wilmington,Del.

MESSAGE: *"Hi Uncle. I was glad to hear from you. I guess you know that Pop is having a sale in a few days. I'm glad to hear that Fred was home. I suppose he had a good time. Here is a little extra meat which isn't rationed. Well, take care of yourself and let me hear from you. A pal. Bill."*

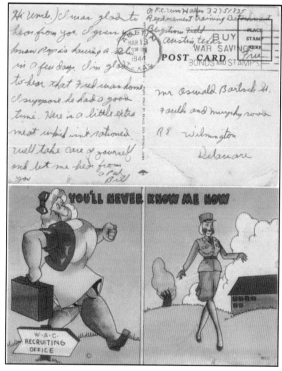

In March of 1944, William K. (Bill) Halfen sent a postcard to his uncle, Oswald Bartsch, Sr., in Wilmington, Del. I found the card one Sunday afternoon in March of 2012 at an antique store in Olney, Maryland.

It's impossible to know how the card got to the antique store, but I have a theory. The woman who owned the shop told me she "bought into" a huge postcard collection from "a house full of paper" in Pennsylvania many years earlier. I suspect Bill Halfen's card was sold in an estate sale when his Uncle Oswald passed away in 1952, then found its way to the "house full of paper," and from there to Olney.

When I started searching for Bill or his children, it didn't take long to find them. Bill had lived in Sykesville, Md., and passed away in 2005. (Sykesville is about 20 miles from Olney, which make me wonder if Bill ever passed by the antique store where his postcard languished for all those years.) I found Bill's obituary, which listed a son, Ken, in the Baltimore area. Ken was easy to find through his profile on Linked In. I got an address and sent him a snail mail letter. Two days later Ken sent me an email:

"I received your letter today regarding the postcard my father wrote. Yes!!! I would love to have it. Thank you. My parents passed away 7 years ago, and I have much of their history. My father was not a

Bill Halfen during World War II

38

prolific writer because he was embarrassed of never having had a good education or good handwriting. But, I have many letters and cards he wrote to my mother when he was in WWII, and I cherish them. I applaud your efforts and compassion in doing this."

I sent him the card, and Ken and I struck up an email friendship. Ken was kind enough to send a photograph of his parents holding his son, Zack, taken when Zack was four months old. Bill was past 80 when Zack was born, giving him a bonus late-in-life grandson. Norman Rockwell himself could not have captured the joy of grandparenthood any better than that photograph of Bill and Ruth Halfen with their grandson. With his wizened face and wire-rimmed glasses slipping down his nose, Bill epitomizes the grandfather any child would be lucky to have.

In our email exchanges, Ken sounded a theme I hear almost every time I contact the children of a World War II veteran: "Dad had an interesting life, but nothing glamorous. He never brought attention to himself, but would always help someone else - a very humble person who made an impression on me."

Bill was not the only military man from the Halfen family. His brother, Peter, enlisted in late 1945 and had a career in the Air

Bill and Ruth Halfen with grandson, Zack.

Force, retiring as a Master Sergeant.

Most postcards marketed to soldiers during the war had humorous images of Army life or a patriotic theme. This particular card was labeled, "You'll Never Know Me Now," and featured before-and-after drawings of a young woman who joined the WACs (Women's Army Corp).

In the "before" version she is an extremely plump girl with Popeye forearms and ham-hock calves, looking like she just fell off the turnip truck. She's striding toward the WAC Recruiting Office, battered suitcase in hand. In the "after" view she's a gorgeous woman with an hourglass figure accentuated by a tailored uniform; long, slim legs; and a chic hairstyle.

Bill's comment on the card is priceless: "Here is a little extra meat which isn't rationed."

Try it. It's fun. (Taking A Bath In A Steel Helmet)

FROM: PFC Bob Carrucci; Camp San Luis Obispo, Calif.; Sept. 28, 1945

TO: His wife Betty, back home in Brooklyn.

IMAGE: Drab Army camp.

MESSAGE: *"Hello honey. We stopped near this town yesterday on our way down here. It was very cold on the way down and when we got up this morning, but now it is very hot out. How is everything back home coming along? How has the weather been at home? I don't know how long I'll be around but will get in touch with you. All my love, Bob."*

FROM: PFC Bob Carrucci; Camp Blanding, Fla.; July 29, 1945

TO: "The Gang" at Frank A. Carrucci Construction Co. in Brooklyn

IMAGE: Alluring bathing beauty languishing on the beach.

MESSAGE: *"Hello Gang: We're away for two weeks in a battle bivouac* (illegible). *I set my tent up Monday night and slept in it once so far. The picture on this card isn't a sample of the "battles" I've been in. The only adventure I've been in is trying to take a bath in a steel helmet, with a pint of water, shaving and then wash your feet and socks in the same water. Try it, it's fun. Regards to all, Bob."*

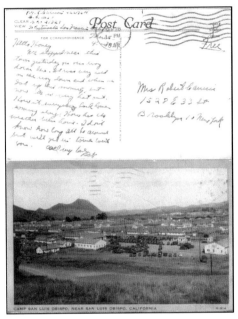

Robert John (Bob) Carucci was well on his way to an established life in Brooklyn when the Army called him to service at age 28. The son of Italian immigrants, Bob was married and a construction foreman at a family-owned contracting company when he entered the Army in April 1945. I learned of Bob though two very different postcards he wrote in July and September of that year.

In September 1945 he sent his wife Betty (Elizabeth Tye Carucci) a card that pictured an Army base at San Luis Obispo, California. The message was the usual chatty update:

"Hello Honey:

"We stopped near this town on our way down here. It was very cold on the way down and when we got up this morning, but now it is very hot out. How is everything back home coming along? How has the weather been at home? I don't know how long I'll be around but will get in touch with you.

"All my love, Bob."

Bob's postcard to Betty featured a nondescript photo of an Army camp, but the card he wrote to the guys back at Frank A. Carucci Contracting in Brooklyn had a different theme. The card was postmarked July 14, 1945, from Camp Blanding, Fla., about 50 miles inland from St. Augustine. Labeled "Blond Adventuress," the card featured an alluring blond in a skimpy swimsuit lounging on the beach. He wrote:

"Hello Gang:

"We're away for two weeks in a battle bivouac (illegible). I set my tent up Monday night and slept in it once so far. The picture on this card isn't a sample of the "battles" I've been in. The only adventure I've been in is trying to take a bath in a steel helmet, with a pint of water, shaving and then wash your feet and socks in the same water. Try it, it's fun.

"Regards to all, Bob."

Tracking down Bob Carucci's story was one of my most challenging efforts. After many dead ends I learned that Bob and Elizabeth died with no surviving relatives. I found very little information about where Bob served in the Army or his life after the war. All I've been able to learn about him comes from an obituary published when he died of Parkinson's disease at age 85 in 2002 in Sarasota, Fla.

Bob returned home after the war, earned a degree from Polytechnic University in Brooklyn (probably with help from the GI Bill), and owned Carucci Contracting Company until he retired in 1980. During his retirement in Florida he belonged to the Elks Lodge, Palm Aire Country Club, the American Legion, and a Catholic church.

Elizabeth passed away in 2007 at age 90. Her obituary poignantly reported, "There are no known survivors. She leaves behind three healthgivers, Janine, Raul and Nika. She was preceded in death by husband, Robert, and daughter, Lorrie. She was a member of St. Thomas More Catholic Church. She was the first woman chapter chairperson for the American Red Cross. Elizabeth was a wonderful friend to many."

Two people who posted comments to her online obituary described a caring couple. One said, "(Betty) was a wonderful, caring, vibrant woman and was loved by all. Always ready with a laugh and a smile . She will be missed." Another said Bob and Elizabeth "… would do anything for anyone and were especially nice to my entire family."

Most of the postcards I research from soldiers in World War II led me to their Baby Boomer children. With no surviving children, Bob and Elizabeth Carucci left a different legacy. Their estate included bequests of more than $50,000 each to New College in Sarasota and to the New York City YMCA.

My Beloved, I'll Never Forget It So Long As I Live

FROM: Veronica Anderson; New York City; July and August 1942

TO: Staff Sgt. Howard Anderson, her future husband; Camp Livingston, La.

MESSAGE:

(Penn Station card) – *"My beloved. Do you remember the day we parted here. I'll never forget it so long as I live. I actually see you here every day when coming to work. I love you. Your own, Ronnie."*

(AWOL soldier card) – *"Dear Howie. Hope you are feeling well and the weather is not too warm. I hope you are not doing what the soldier on this card has done. Everyone sends their love. Always, Ronnie."*

(Buck Private card) – *"Darling. Hope you are doing well. How's your (illegible)? Very rainy day today and pretty cool. How's everything at camp, angel? Everyone sends their regards to you. Hope you like the humor of this card. I love you. Your own, Ronnie."*

If you're ever at Penn Station in New York City, think about this wartime love story of Veronica and Howard.

Railroads were the primary mode of transportation for millions of people during World War II. Many a sad farewell was said at train stations in big cities and small towns. One such parting took place at the landmark Penn Station in New York when a young woman named Veronica (nicknamed Ronnie) said good-bye to her soldier boyfriend, Howard.

He went off to Camp Livingston, La., and she stayed at her job in New York. We'll never know how often she sent him a postcard, but it might have been every day. I found three cards she sent during just one week in July 1942.

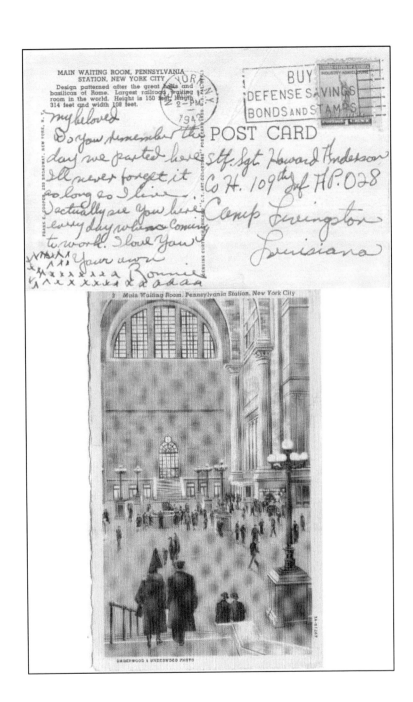

MAIN WAITING ROOM, PENNSYLVANIA
STATION, NEW YORK CITY
Design patterned after the great halls and
basilicas of Rome. Largest railroad waiting
room in the world. Height is 150 feet, length
314 feet and width 108 feet.

POST CARD

my beloved
Do you remember the
day we parted here
I'll never forget it
so long as I live
I actually see you here
every day when coming
to work. I love you
Your own
Bonnie
xxxxxxxxxxx

Stf. Sgt. Howard Anderson
Co H. 109th Inf A.P.O.28
Camp Livingston
Louisiana

BUY
DEFENSE SAVINGS
BONDS AND STAMPS

3 Main Waiting Room, Pennsylvania Station, New York City

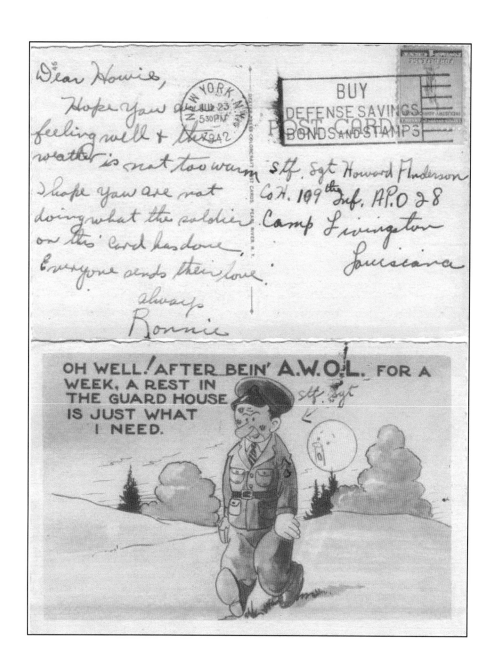

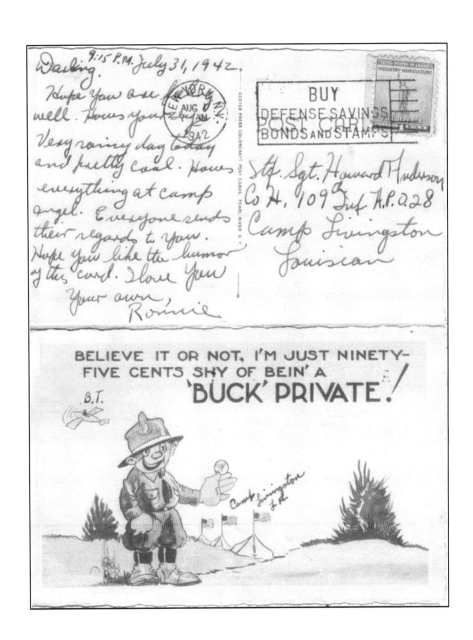

One of the cards featured a photo of the main waiting room at Penn Station. The message said:

"My beloved,

"Do you remember the day we parted here? I'll never forget it so long as I live. I actually see you here every day when coming to work. I love you.

"Your own, Ronnie"

Just before I acquired this postcard, Becky and I took the train from our home in Frederick, Maryland, to New York for the Macy's parade, arriving and departing through Penn Station. The original station is gone now, but when I saw that postcard of the grand old waiting room I conjured an image of Ronnie still seeing Howard there every day on her way to work.

As I read the card I wondered about these young lovers. Were they married at the time? If not, did they get married? Did he make it through the war alive? Did they ever see each other again?

This card was one of three from Ronnie to Howard that I acquired from an eBay seller in Pennsylvania. The other two were equally loving, but also humorous. One depicted an AWOL soldier with lipstick smears on his face. Ronnie wrote, "I hope you are not doing what the soldier on this card has done." The other showed a sloppily dressed soldier holding a nickel and saying, "I'm just 95 cents shy of being a Buck Private." Her note said, "Hope you like the humor of this card." She personalized the cards with her own doodles. On one of them she inserted the label "Camp Livingston," Howard's post at the time. The cartoon on the card included an airplane. She inexplicably labeled the pilot "B.T." Perhaps "B.T." was a friend who was an aviator.

My search for Ronnie and Howard was not easy. I knew his name was Howard Anderson, but there was no middle initial or service number on the postcard. When I searched the National Archives database of World War II enlistments I found 294 soldiers named Howard Anderson.

Next I tried finding Ronnie. I assumed her name was Veronica, and if they were married she would be Veronica Anderson. A Google search for Veronica Anderson produced 88,000 results. I gave up and put the card in my "too tough" file.

A few weeks later I discovered a search feature on the Archives database I had overlooked. It's possible to search for soldiers by their state of residence. One of the cards was addressed to Howard at a unit of the Pennsylvania National Guard, so I presumed he was from Pennsylvania. Using the search feature I found 15 Howard Andersons who enlisted from Pennsylvania. That was still too many to find this particular Howard Anderson, so the card went back in the "too tough" file.

Then it hit me. The Archives database also lists "Source of Army Personnel." Most of the men who enlisted came from "Civil Life" or "Regular Army," but a few were from "National Guard." Only one of the 15 Howard Andersons from Pennsylvania came from the National Guard. His name was Howard D. Anderson. Once I knew the middle initial it didn't take long to find him through an obituary in a California newspaper:

"Howard Dewitt Anderson, 91, of Sonoma, died June 6, 2004, at his home in Sonoma.

"Mr. Anderson was born in Brooklyn, N.Y., and was a decorated veteran, serving in the U.S. Army in World War II. He was a painter and wallpaper hanger for 25 years, and was a wood craftsman his entire life. He was a 43-year resident of Sonoma.

"Mr. Anderson was the dear husband of Veronica L. Anderson."

Next I found Ronnie's obituary:

"Veronica Louise Anderson a longtime resident of Sonoma and a native of New York, passed away on her birthday, October 27, 2006, she was 87. She was born in New York and married Howard D. Anderson on January 25, 1943. They were married until his death on June 4, 2004.

"She was an active member of St. Francis Solano Catholic Church and volunteered as one of the "Hot Dog Ladies" at the School lunch program and volunteered at the bake sales as well. She often cooked meals for the Nuns and Priests including Father Roberts, who the

church hall is named for. Before moving to Sonoma, she worked as a florist in New York."

I was never able to contact any family members to return the postcard, but on Findagrave I located the final chapter in the love story of Ronnie and Howard – a photo of a gravestone in the St. Francis Solano Cemetery in Sonoma, Calif., with their names inscribed together. From the obituaries and gravestone I was able to piece together a little of the puzzle. When Ronnie wrote the postcards in the summer of 1942, she was 22 and Howard was 29. They were not yet married; they wed January 25, 1943. It appears Howard was in combat and wounded during the war, as his gravestone shows he received the Bronze Star Medal and Purple Heart.

"Your own Ronnie" and "My beloved" Howard" are buried together in Sonoma, California

The mystery was solved. "My beloved" Howard did indeed return safely from the war and enjoyed more than 60 years of marriage to "Your own, Ronnie." When I saw the gravestone photo I recalled her line from the postcard, "I'll never forget it so long as I live." I like to believe that in the final years of her life, after Howard was gone, Ronnie would sometimes dream of that long-ago farewell at Penn Station as she drifted off to sleep.

Having Grand Time, See You Next Weekend

FROM: Staff Sgt. Russell Liddle and his bride Betty; honeymooning at Ocean Grove, N.J., July 14, 1942

TO: His relatives in Williamstown, Mass.

MESSAGE: *"Lane and Lill – LL. Having grand time. See you next week end. Love, Betty and Russ"*

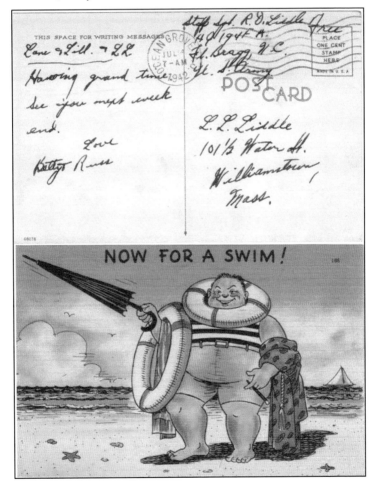

52

Staff Sgt. Russell Dewain Liddle, Sr. married Bessie May (Betty) Hillebrand on July 11, 1942. Three days later they sent a brief postcard to Russell's brother Lane and his wife Lillian in Williamstown, Mass. The card was postmarked July 14, 1942, from Ocean Grove, N.J., and the return address was Staff Sgt. R. D. Liddle, Ft. Bragg, N.C. The card said:

> *"Lane and Lill – LL*
> *"Having grand time. See you next week end.*
> *"Love, Betty and Russ"*

I acquired the card from an eBay seller in New Jersey. It caught my eye because it was not the typical military card. Instead of a cartoon about Army life it was a beach scene depicting a portly man in a swimsuit, laden with paraphernalia and saying, "Now for a swim."

While it had taken me months to find Howard and Ronnie Anderson, I found the Liddles within an hour. Russ put his middle initial in the return address, which helped narrow down the search. Liddle is not a common name, and I quickly

Russell and Betty Liddle on their wedding day in July 1942.

found a family history web site created by Russell's son Mark. The web site even included a photo of Russell and Betty on their wedding day.

Using an email address from the Liddle family web site I sent Mark Liddle a message. He replied soon thereafter, and I sent him the card written by his parents 70 years earlier.

The wartime marriage of Russ and Betty Liddle lasted more than 60 years. He died Jan. 26, 2004, and she passed away Nov. 6, 2005. They had five children, and when Russ died they had 16 grandchildren and 12 great-grandchildren.

Like thousands of World War II couples, Russ and Betty raised a family, lived productive lives, and contributed to their community. As recounted in his obituary, Russell Liddle:

"... was a World War II Veteran with the 194th Field Artillery Battalion of the U.S. Army in the European Theatre of Operations having served in North Africa, Naples-Foggia, Rome-Arno, Anzio and in the Rhineland Campaigns.

"He was employed at Brady & Palmer Printing Co. in New York for 40 years until his retirement in 1984.

"Mr. Liddle was a member of the Masonic Lodge 992 of Queens Village, member of St. Michael's Episcopal Church, VFW and American Legion and also a member of the 40 & 8 Club of the American Legion all of New York. He was also a Scoutmaster in New York City."

The account of his military service shows that Russ Liddle served in the same places in Italy as two of my other "postcard people:" Clark McWilliams, whose ill-fated B-24 took off from Foggia; and Adolph Hunecke who died at Anzio.

Betty's obituary also recounts a life of family, work, and service:

"Prior to moving to Maine in 1998, she resided in New York where she had worked as a mental therapist at the Harlem Valley Psychiatric Center. She also taught Sunday School at St. Joseph's Episcopal Church in Queen's Village, N.Y. She was a den mother, a Girl Scout leader, and a member of the senior group of Pine Bush, N.Y."

When Mark Liddle wrote to me concerning his parents' postcard, he summed up the sentiment I hear from many of the "postcard families:"

54

"Thank you so much for the image. That was very kind. ... My parents died in 2004 and 2005. They really were great and were loved."

Mother: I Thought This Card Might Make You A Little Bit Happier

FROM: A soldier named Harold; Baton Rouge, La.; April 17, 1942

TO: His mother back home in Wisconsin

MESSAGE: *"Dear Mother: I just wrote you a letter this morning, but thought this card might make you a little bit happier and show you that I think of you all the time. Tell Dad I think of him at the same time. I'll send a card as often as I see one that is worth sending. Lovingly, Harold."*

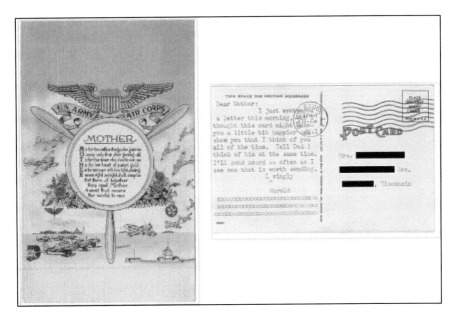

    While my goal is to return postcards to the families of soldiers who wrote them, I sometimes come across a card so compelling I want to share its story even though the trail went cold. One such card was written by a young soldier named Harold to his mother in 1942.

    A Milwaukee native born in 1919, Harold was the eldest son of German-born parents. He enlisted in the Army in late January 1942, less than two months after Pearl Harbor. According to his enlistment record he was a high school graduate, single with no dependents, and employed

56

as a "Code 727 semiskilled painters, construction and maintenance workers."

On April 17, 1942, three months after joining the Army, he sent his mother a postcard from Baton Rouge, La. I suspect Harold was a company clerk (like Radar O'Reilly from M*A*S*H) because the card is neatly typewritten with perfect grammar and punctuation

The card features the insignia of the Army Air Corps and images of airplanes. In the center of the card, surrounded by roses, is the "Mother" poem ("M" is for the million things she gave me, etc.). I wondered if Harold had to conceal the card from his Army buddies so they wouldn't razz him for being a "mama's boy." The card says:

"Dear Mother:

"I just wrote you a letter this morning, but thought this card might make you a little bit happier and show you that I think of you all the time. Tell Dad I think of him at the same time. I'll send a card as often as I see one that is worth sending.

"Lovingly, Harold."

Except for the enlistment data and the postcard, I know very little about Harold. He died at age 36 in 1955, years before his mother passed away in 1979. I'm not using his surname, since I was unable to find any family members. Someday I might learn more about Harold, find his family and return his postcard to a relative. Despite hitting a dead end in my search, I'm touched by the thoughtfulness of a son who sent his mother such a sentimental card.

Pull The String Of The Flag For Men In Service

FROM: Maj. S. Howard Cohan, Army dentist; Camp Edwards, Mass.;
Oct. 29, 1942

TO: His daughter, Joann, in Bridgeport, Conn.

MESSAGE: *"Darling Joann: I plan to come home late Saturday night. Glad to hear Corky was picked to pull the string of the flag for men in the service. Feel much better, thank you. Love, Daddy."*

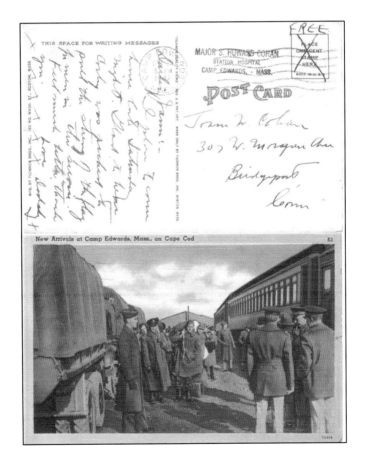

New Arrivals at Camp Edwards, Mass., on Cape Cod

Military service in World War II brought together people from all backgrounds, occupations, and educational levels. The postcards I found reflect that diversity. Most were written by men with a high school education who worked with their hands -- auto workers, house painters, farmers, coal miners. Then there's Major S. Howard Cohan, a dentist from Connecticut.

The first thing I noticed about his postcard was the return address. On all my other postcards the return address is hastily scribbled and often barely legible. By contrast, Howard Cohan's return address was affixed with a rubber stamp:

Major S. Howard Cohan
Station Hospital
Camp Edwards, Mass.

Dated Oct. 29, 1942, the card was addressed to his 14-year-old daughter Joann Cohan in Bridgeport, Conn. One side of the card is a photo of "New Arrivals at Camp Edwards," showing men in uniform getting off a train and preparing to board Army trucks. The message side of the card said:

"Darling Joann:

"I plan to come home late Saturday night. Glad to hear Corky was picked to pull the string of the flag for men in the service. Feel much better, thank you.

"Love, Daddy"

I learned that "Corky" was Joann's younger sister, Rosamond. I presume "pull the string of the flag" meant Corky was chosen at school one day to raise the flag in honor of men in the military. One can also surmise from the wording that Joann had written to her father and that he had been ailing but now felt better.

Many of the people whose postcards I researched were hard to find; not so the Cohan family. In searching the web I found engagement and wedding announcements for Joann and Corky in Connecticut newspapers. By knowing Joann's married name (Joann Cohan Robin) I was able to find several online references to the sisters and their spouses, including Joann's obituary when she died in 2007. Among her survivors was a son, David Robin. Through Google searches I learned he's a physicist at Lawrence Berkeley National Laboratory in California, which means his name frequently appears in technical papers and conference programs. (It also means he's *really, really* smart.) I found David's email address and sent him a note. He replied a few hours later:

> *"Dear John,*

> *"What a wonderful and unexpected surprise! Howard was my grandfather, Joann my mother and Corky was my aunt. Joann passed away 5 years ago and Corky just last month. I would love to have a copy of the card. I would share it with my sister Debbie and cousins.*

> *"Now that Corky has passed away there is no one left in the family that has direct memories of this period. This is a very thoughtful thing that you have done.*

> *"Best Wishes, Dave"*

As I began to "pull the string" on this postcard, I discovered a remarkably accomplished family. Dr. Cohan, born in 1897, was in his forties when he penned the postcard to Joann in 1942, older than most American servicemen. Joann, the 14-year-old girl who received the postcard from "Daddy," went on to be a well-known music therapist, as noted in her obituary:

> *"Joann was one of the pioneers in the field of music therapy, having entered the field in 1947 upon graduating from Connecticut College as a music major, elected to Phi Beta Kappa. Among the institutions she was associated with were Payne Whitney Clinic of New York Hospital, Cornell Medical Center, Yale Psychiatric Institute of New Haven, Conn., and the West Haven Veterans Administration Hospital. She was associated with many other institutions, establishing some music therapy programs for the first time. She also lectured widely on music therapy, including invited lectures abroad in Japan and Australia. She found great satisfaction in using music to help others get well or at least make a better adjustment to life."*

Joann's husband, Richard Shale Robin, held a doctoral degree from Harvard, was a long-time professor of philosophy at Mount Holyoke College, lectured throughout the world, and co-founded the Society for the Advancement of American Philosophy. As noted above, their son David is an accelerator physicist at Lawrence Berkeley Lab.

Corky, who passed away in 2012, was also a musician, having earned an undergraduate degree at Vassar and a master's at Smith College. She was a professor of music history at University of London. Her first husband was a professor of philosophy at Oxford, and her second husband a professor of music in Scotland.

In addition to the family's numerous accomplishments, another fact about Dr. Cohan impressed me. According to the 1930 census, his parents were born in Russia. This son of immigrants became a dentist, his daughters and their spouses were accomplished musicians and professors, and his grandson is a scientist at a national laboratory.

To top off this American success story, Dr. Cohan, just like the "Yankee Doodle Dandy" in the famous song written by another man named Cohan, was born on the Fourth of July.

I Waited Too Long And Now It's Too Late To Ask

Three soldiers from Maine sent postcards to Alice Knox and her daughter, Ella Merrill, in Livermore Falls, Maine, in 1942. The soldiers were Raymond Merrill and Clifton Eames of Livermore Falls, and Francis Folsom of Monmouth. When I purchased the cards in an antique store in Colorado they sparked my interest in World War II postcards. On the following pages are two cards from Clifton Eames, two from Francis Folsom, and three from Raymond Merrill. I located daughters of Clifton Eames and Francis Folsom and returned the cards to them. Raymond Merrill apparently had no descendants.

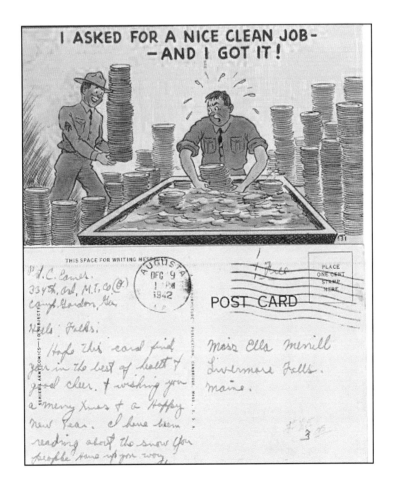

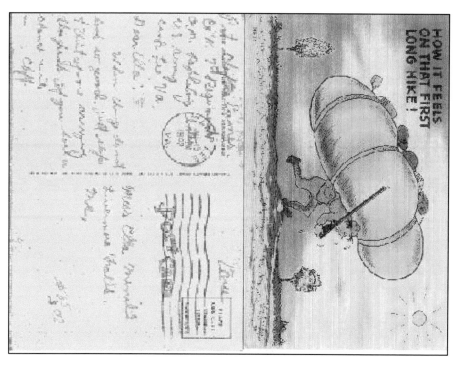

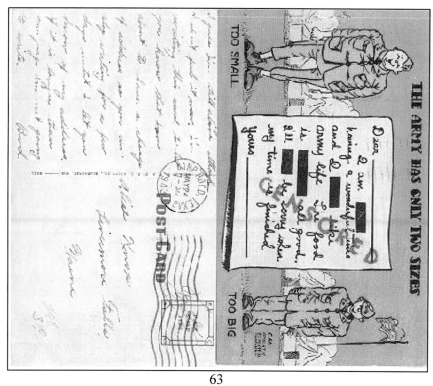

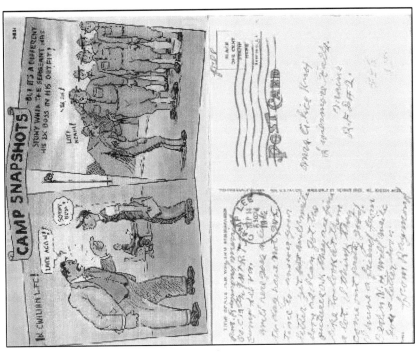

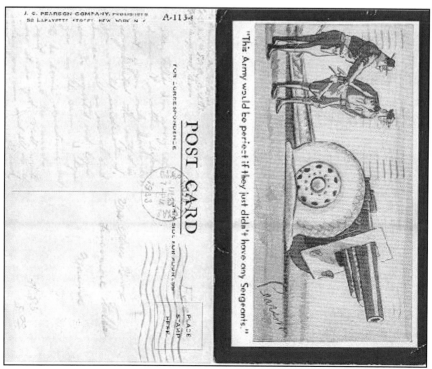

Livermore Falls is a small town along the Androscoggin River in Maine. When the war started, Raymond Merrill and Clifton Eames were young men living on farms outside town. Raymond's aunt, Alice Knox, and her daughter, Ella Merrill, lived together nearby. Raymond's cousin, Francis Merrill Folsom, lived about 30 miles away in Monmouth.

Raymond and Clifton went into the Army a few months apart in 1942. Francis enlisted in February 1943, just after his 19th birthday.

All three men wrote to Alice and Ella at various times. Clifton sent cards in July of 1942, a month after enlisting, and again in December. Raymond sent three cards, two in the fall of 1942 and another in March of 1943. Francis corresponded with Alice and Ella in May and July of 1943.

When I bought the cards in 2003 at an antique store in Colorado, internet genealogical resources were in their early stages. I could find a little information about the men, but not enough to locate them or their descendants. I put the cards in a cigar box, and there they stayed for eight years while I moved from Colorado to Kentucky to Maryland.

I renewed my search in 2011, and with the maturation of sites like Ancestry and Findagrave it didn't take long to find information about Clifton and Raymond. My satisfaction in finally solving the Livermore Falls mystery was dampened by what I learned about Raymond. In searching for him on Ancestry I came across a death certificate showing he hanged himself at Camp Mackall, N.C., in May of 1943, nine months after joining the Army. His body was returned to Livermore Falls for burial.

CLIFTON EAMES

In looking for Clifton Eames I lost several months pursuing a false lead, discovering much to my amazement that there were two unrelated people named Clifton Eames in Maine during that period. Once I started searching for the correct Clifton Eames it was relatively easy to locate his daughter, Leola Keene, and return Clifton's two cards to her. Mrs. Keene wrote back, enclosing a photo of her father and describing his military service:

"Dad was a Parts Clerk, Automotive, who started his tour of Europe at Normandy, Northern France, Rhineland, Ardennes, Central Europe. As most vets, Dad rarely talked about the service experience. Dad had a respect for then Gen. Eisenhower. Dad had a number of photos of Eisenhower with his troops.

"One of my memories is the comment of a vet who serviced with Dad stating that Dad was able to use humor to break tension and help others deal with difficult situations."

At age 31 when he entered the Army, Clifton Eames was older than most recruits.

Clifton went back to Maine after the war. In 1947 he married Winnifred, a widow whose first husband had died in a motor vehicle accident in Maine. Clifton died in 1975, and Winnifred passed away in 2005 at the age of 92.

I'll probably never know exactly how this batch of World War II postcards got from a house in Maine to an antique store in Colorado, but Mrs. Keene provided a clue. She believes Ella Merrill (later Ella Beckler) took the cards with her when she moved to Indiana around 2001 to live with a daughter. I suspect the cards were sold at an estate sale when Ella passed away at age 91 in 2003.

FRANCIS FOLSOM

The last piece of the Livermore Falls puzzle fell into place when I found the story of Francis Folsom. I determined he died in 1997 and located his daughter, Christine Bearce, a teacher and assistant principal in Gorham, Maine. I sent her the cards written by her father (and those from Raymond Merrill, since he and her father were cousins). My letter to her elicited the following email:

67

"First off, thank you so much for taking the time to research the post cards and trying to connect them to family members. You absolutely made my day and then some. Francis M. Folsom is my dad and he passed away 13 years ago. I dearly miss him and seeing copies of his postcards to his Aunt Alice is very emotional for me. I hope you have guessed that I would love to have the postcards."

In letters to families, I sometimes describe my postcard hobby as a way to "keep me off the street." In her reply, Mrs. Bearce said:

"You have found a very worthwhile way to stay busy and 'off the street.'"

Just like Ken Halfen who is quoted in another chapter, Christine spoke of her father's quiet modesty.

"He was a pretty average man, but very special to me and my sisters. I have his Purple Heart and one picture of him in his uniform."

In a follow-up email, Mrs. Bearce provided more information about her father's World War II service. She included a photo of her dad, a ruggedly handsome man.

Francis Folsom at home in Maine before shipping out for combat in Europe.

"He told me he flew to Europe with many soldiers crowded into a cargo plane and when he returned it was on a ship. He stepped on a land mine in France and was brought back to the United States to recover from shrapnel damage to his foot and leg.

"From the postcards you have found, I now know that he was stationed in Fort Hood, Texas, where many troops were in 1943 preparing to go to Europe when needed. My Dad's cards sound like he was overwhelmed by the size of the base and how unsure he was of his fate.

"The picture I will send you is not dated, but I am sure that it was taken in Maine before he went to France. His toes on his injured foot would not have fit into the boots he is wearing in the picture.

"After being in a military hospital he returned to Maine and met and married my mother, Clenda Piper in 1946. They had three daughters, Joyce, Cheryl and me, and were married until his death in 1997. He was an auto mechanic in a city near Monmouth for 12 years and then opened his own garage, Folsom's Filling Station, in Monmouth in 1958. He worked there several years before becoming the Rural Letter Carrier in Monmouth until his retirement. In his retirement he built gift store souvenirs, then he became the handyman/greenskeeper for the local golf club. He built furniture, made trail markers for the snowmobile club out of recycled soda cans and maintained a large garden. He was a busy man; he always worked hard and would say yes whenever someone needed help. I never remember him saying a negative thing about another person and his nickname, Buddy, was perfect for him. He was not 'great' but I believe he was an exceptionally 'good' man."

She closed with a poignant line that rings true for many of us who have lost our parents:

"He talked very little of his military experience and only if we asked him specific questions. Like many people I waited too long and now it's too late to ask."

A Son Lost In Battle, A War Bride Lost In Time

FROM: Private (later Captain) David Morton; sent from Tennessee; circa 1942

TO: His little sister "Beanie" in Jessups, Maryland

MESSAGE: *"Hello Beanie. Just a line to say hello and to let you know I'll only be here about a week or 10 days more. I don't believe they are giving any more furloughs. If I go for pilot, I will be at Maxwell Field on the 15th, and if I go for bombardier I will go to California any day now. Say hello to everybody for me. Love, Dave."*

This card with the "Stripe Happy Guy" must have been popular with the troops. It is one of the cards I often see for sale on eBay.

The Morton family of Jessup, Md. sent three sons (Charlie, David, and Howard) and a daughter (Albina) to the service during World War II. David, who married while stationed in Wales, was killed when his plane went down during the Battle of the Bulge. The Morton family not only lost a son, but also lost track of his "war bride" after briefly meeting her in 1946.

The four Morton siblings are all dead now, but family members still honor their memory and still search for David's long lost bride. Succeeding generations of the family have continued serving our country, most recently with three young men who fought in Iraq and Afghanistan.

Capt. David Morton (right), a pilot, was killed when his plane was shot down during the Battle of the Bulge.

The postcard that led me to this notable family was written by David Morton and addressed to his sister, Albina ("Beanie"), back home in Jessup. She later became an Army nurse. No one knows when David wrote the card or whether it actually reached Albina. Although he wrote his return address (an Air Corps base in Nashville) on the card and put the word "Free" in lieu of a stamp, there's no postmark to show the card was mailed. There are several possible explanations. Maybe the card somehow escaped being postmarked by the Post Office. Maybe he decided to mail a batch of cards in an envelope. Maybe he got an unexpected leave and delivered it in person. Maybe he forgot to mail it and the card somehow ended up in an auction many years later.

While the card is undated, the content suggests he wrote it in the spring of 1942. He enlisted in late 1941 and had apparently just finished

71

basic training at the time he wrote to Beanie. He was about to start his next phase of training to be either a pilot or bombardier. The card said:

"Hello Beanie,

"Just a line to say hello and to let you know I'll only be here about a week or 10 days more. I don't believe they are giving any more furloughs. If I go for pilot, I will be at Maxwell Field on the 15th, and if I go for bombardier I will go to California any day now. Say hello to everybody for me.

"Love, Dave."

According to David's enlistment record from the National Archives, he joined the Army on December 10, 1941, three days after Pearl Harbor and 12 days after his 17th birthday. He was one of the many young men who enlisted right after FDR's "date that shall live in infamy" speech. His enlistment file says he had three years of high school, raising the possibility he dropped out of school to join the Army.

He became a pilot and was killed in a crash on Dec. 27, 1944. I easily found that information on

"Beanie," Capt. David Morton's sister Albina, was an Army nurse.

several web sites, and found a photo of his headstone in Baltimore National Cemetery on Findagrave. What I found next was intriguing.

Along with the photo of his headstone on Findagrave I noticed a picture posted by someone named Christina. It shows an officer in dress uniform standing in front of a stone building, arm-in-arm with a beautiful young woman who is wearing a suit with a flower on the lapel. I assumed it was a wedding picture. Closer inspection showed the woman is holding a pair of gloves, just like my mom in her 1943 wedding photo, and there's a shiny wedding band on her left ring finger.

The Findagrave profile for "Christina" led me to contact Christina Morton-Scott via email. She replied almost immediately, and I learned the story behind the photograph. The officer in the photo was David Morton, Christina's great-uncle. The beautiful young woman at

72

his side was Elaine Jessica McGrath of Trethomas, Wales. They were married June 15, 1944, nine days after D-Day. Before that momentous year was over David was killed in action when his plane went down two days after Christmas.

David Morton and his Welsh bride, Elaine Jessica McGrath. Photo was likely taken on their wedding day, June 15, 1944. He was killed in action six months later.

Until I read about David and Elaine I had no idea how many "war brides" came to America after World War II. By some accounts more than 70,000 brides and their children were transported during "Operation War Bride" in which a flotilla of ships (including the Queen Mary) ferried them across the Atlantic. The War Brides Act of 1945 streamlined immigration rules, the Army managed transportation, and the Red Cross assisted the families.

Most of those trips ended with joyous reunions between the war brides and their American husbands. Not so for Elaine, as recounted in a newspaper article published in the Welsh newspaper "Western Mail" in 1946. The headline read, "Welsh Widow Kept Secret Sorrow."

"After many months in hospital following the shock of the death of her husband, Captain David Morton, a troop carrier pilot of the American Air Force, in the Battle of the Bulge, on December 27th, 1944,

Mrs. Elaine Morton, of Trethomas has arrived at the home of her husband's parents, Mr. and Mrs. Charles Morton, of Jessup, Maryland.

"She sailed alone in her cabin on the United States liner Washington, too sensitive to tell any but one of the 649 wives who went with her that she had no husband to meet her when she arrived in America. 'I didn't want sympathy from anybody,' said Mrs. Morton, a former Army Territorial Services pay clerk, who had been married for only 4 months to Captain Morton. In a letter home Mrs. Morton stated that when she arrived at Pennsylvania Station she was met by her father-in-law and received a hearty welcome, which was 'crowned with a warm kiss,' she added.

"Mrs. Morton is the daughter of Mr. and Mrs. George McGrath of James Street, Trethomas."

In my email exchanges with Christina she told me the family lost track of Elaine after their meeting in 1946. They think she may have gone to see relatives in New York, but can't confirm that she actually went there or that she even had relatives in the States. Over the years Christina posted messages on genealogy web sites and took other measures to look for Elaine, all to no avail. If Elaine is still living she would be approaching age 90 years of age.

In nearly every family one person is the "keeper of the keys." Christina has that role in the Morton family, keeping records and photos going back to the mid-1800s. She relates:

"There's a lot of military history in my family, four straight generations starting with my grandfather's generation. My dad was in the Army, 101st Airborne. I'm an Air Force veteran. Three of my four sons are Army. My oldest served two tours in Iraq, my second son served one tour in Iraq, and my youngest son was in Afghanistan for the past year and just returned back to his duty station in Colorado, two weeks ago! Whew!! Now I can de-stress!! Everyone returned home safe and sound!!"

The poignant story of Captain David Morton and Elaine raises more questions than it answers. How did they meet? Since their wedding was only eight days after D-Day, did they decide on the spur of the moment to get married because he was about to ship out for Europe after the Normandy invasion? Did he fly during the D-Day invasion then hurry back to Wales for a quick wedding? What happened to Elaine? Did she return to Wales? Remarry? Have children?

The matter of the missing postmark on David's postcard raises another question. Christina says she can't imagine Beanie or her family discarding such a keepsake. She wonders if Elaine somehow came into possession of the card and her family eventually let it go. I backtracked to the eBay seller, and he provided the name of the auction house where he got the postcard. I passed that information along to Christina.

The answer to the question, "Whatever happened to Elaine?" is out there somewhere. I believe Christina will find it one of these days. When she does, I hope she'll let me know.

16 From This Vicinity Listed As Recent Casualties In War

FROM: Private Adolph Hunecke; Station Hospital, Greenville, Pa.; July 14, 1943

TO: Mrs. Helen Schlather; a family friend; St. Louis, Mo.

MESSAGE: *"Hello Mrs. Schlather and boys. I received a letter from Leonard about a month ago. I will be home about July 24. Tell everyone hello. Regards, Buddy."*

When deciding whether to acquire a postcard and look for the writer's family, I usually focus on the name and location. If the writer has a common name like "Joe Smith" and the card was sent to someone in a big city I pass it up, figuring it would be nearly impossible to find the right person. If the writer's name is less common and the card went to a small town the odds are better of finding the family.

A card I found on eBay written by PFC Adolph F. Hunecke passed my "uncommon name" test, but it was sent to someone in St. Louis, hardly a small town. I bought it anyway for various personal reasons. First, the card was addressed to Mrs. Helen Schlather, whose uncommon surname is almost identical to mine (Schlatter). Second, my dad was stationed at Jefferson Barracks in St. Louis during the war, and my mother joined him there after they married in November 1943.

I remember my mother telling tales of living in St. Louis at "Mrs. Buecke's Rooming House" and working in the payroll office of the department store Stix, Baer, and Fuller. The rooming house, at 9833 South Broadway, was about eight miles

Private Adolph Hunecke

from the Hunecke residence. In my active imagination I wonder if my mother or father might have crossed paths with the Hunecke or Schlather families.

The postcard was dated July 14, 1943, with a return address of an Army hospital in Pennsylvania. Enlistment records show Private Hunecke had only been in the Army five months at the time he wrote the postcard. I don't know if he was at the hospital for training, was working there, or was recuperating from an injury.

Finding Private Hunecke was easy, but finding his relatives was not. The National Archives database had only one Adolph Hunecke, inducted February 27, 1943. A Google search revealed he was killed in action January 30, 1944, only 10 months later. From there the trail went cold.

Private Hunecke's enlistment record showed he was married. He was born in 1912, making him 30 at the time he enlisted, old enough to have children. However, I couldn't find an obituary or any other source to show whether he had children. From Ancestry I learned his wife was named Marguerite and his mother was likely named Georgiana, but beyond that I kept hitting dead ends.

Then I got a break. In a broad Google search for "Hunecke" and "St. Louis" I found the following obituary:

"LEIGHTON, GENETTE C. (nee Hunecke) in her 96th year, fortified with the Sacraments of Holy Mother Church, Mon., Nov. 20, 2000; beloved wife of the late Charles F. Leighton, Sr.; loving mother of Charles F. (Nancy) Leighton, Jr. and Joan K. (Joseph) Pfeifer; dear grandmother of Cheryl (Mark) Tiburzi, Andrea (Steven) Richardson, Kathleen and Charles W. Leighton; our dear sister, great-grandmother, aunt and friend."

Since Mrs. Leighton's maiden name was Hunecke I figured she might have been Private Hunecke's sister. Her obituary listed a son, Charles, whose wife's name was Nancy. I found an address for a Charles and Nancy Leighton through St. Louis County property records and, taking a shot in the dark, sent them a letter in early April 2012.

A week later my cell phone rang (I include a phone number with my letters). A pleasant voice said, "Mr. Schlatter, this is Nancy Leighton in St. Louis. We got your letter. My husband, Charles, is Adolph Hunecke's nephew. We're just so excited; we'd love to have the postcard."

Nancy explained she was calling on behalf of her husband because he was ill at the time. She said the family still honors the memory of "Uncle Buddy," as Private Hunecke was called. (He signed his postcard "Buddy.") She said they don't know much about how Uncle Buddy died. A family member got some information from the Army several years ago, and Nancy's recollection was that he was killed at Anzio in Italy. She said Uncle Buddy didn't have children, and the Hunecke family lost track of his widow after the war.

I sent them the postcard, and continued looking for more information. The St. Louis Public Library has an extensive online listing of obituaries from the *Post-Dispatch* newspaper. It showed an obituary for Private Hunecke, with photo, was published March 19, 1944 (about six weeks after he was killed).

The library web site does not contain text of the obituaries, only an index. Through the St. Louis Genealogical Society I found a researcher, Carole Goggin, who for a very reasonable fee found the article and sent me a scanned copy. Carole was very diligent, making two trips to the library to make sure she got a good quality copy for me.

The article was not an individual obituary; rather, it was a report of 16 soldiers from St. Louis who were killed in action at various locations. The first paragraph said:

"Private Adolph Frederick Hunecke, son of Mrs. Georgianna Hunecke, 4626 Tower Grove Place, was killed in action Jan. 30 in Italy, the War Department revealed yesterday. Pvt. Hunecke, 32 years old, was the husband of Mrs. Marguerite Hunecke, 4517 Tower Grove Place. A former welder at the Gimlin Engineering Co., 1133 South Seventh Street, he was inducted into the infantry in February 1943 and was sent overseas four months ago."

ST. LOUIS POST-DISPATCH SUNDAY MORNING, MARCH 19, 1944

Among the Wounded, Killed or Missing

CONNORS   BRANOM   RENNER   RITSCH   JASKIEWICZ

MARIK   PANNIER   HUNECKE   WASSILAK   VOLO

16 From This Vicinity Listed As Recent Casualties in War

Among Them Are Six Airmen Missing in Action and Three Others in Armed Services Killed.

Pvt. Adolph Frederick Hunecke, son of Mrs. Georgianna Hunecke, 4626 Tower Grove place, was killed in action Jan. 30 in Italy, the War Department revealed yesterday. Pvt. Hunecke, 32 years old, was the husband of Mrs. Marguerite Hunecke, 4517 Tower Grove place. A former welder at the Gimlin Engineering Co., 1133 South Seventh street, he was inducted into the infantry in February, 1943, and was sent overseas four months ago.

Ferdinand Schwarz, 134 Virginia avenue, Belleville, has been informed. He was employed at the Belleville Postoffice prior to his enlistment in August, 1942. He has been overseas since last October.

Sgt. Thurman P. Smotherman, 29, waist gunner on a Flying Fortress, has been missing in action over Germany since Feb. 8, his brother, H. D. Smotherman, 3417 North Ninth street, has been informed. He is a son of the Rev. and Mrs. M. P. Smotherman.

That completed the picture for Private Hunecke, but one more piece of the puzzle remained – who was Mrs. Schlather and why did Private Hunecke write to her? I found a few clues. The Hunecke and Schlather addresses were only about a mile apart in St. Louis. The postcard was to "Mrs. Schlather and boys," and it said, "I received a card from Leonard about a month ago."

In the 1920 St. Louis census I found a Schlather family with wife Helen, age 25, and five-year-old son Leonard. Amazingly (at least I think it's amazing) I also found on Ancestry a photo of Leonard Henry Schlather, Bachelor of Laws, in the 1937 yearbook of St. Louis University.

Leonard Schlather and Adolph Hunecke were about the same age and lived in the same neighborhood in St. Louis. It's likely they were friends and Adolph corresponded with Leonard's family during the war. I believe that at some point, probably when Mrs. Schlather died in

1971, the postcard was put in an estate sale, and eventually made its way to me through eBay. I returned it to Private

Private Hunecke's postcard was addressed to the family of Leonard Schlather, shown here in a photo from the 1937 St. Louis University yearbook.

Hunecke's relatives in St. Louis 68 years after it was written.

Private Hunecke is buried at the Jefferson Barracks National Cemetery in St. Louis. Until I began researching this book I was not aware of the large number of remains of American soldiers returned to the United States for burial after the war. I knew the American Battle Monuments Commission (ABMC) administers cemeteries overseas where nearly 100,000 Americans killed during World War II are buried, but I didn't know about remains returned to the States. According to the AMBC, "By the end of World War II, several hundred temporary cemeteries had been established by the American Graves Registration Service of the United States Army. During the years 1947 to 1954 that Service, complying with the expressed wishes of the next of kin, and by authority of law, repatriated the remains of some 172,000 recovered bodies."

I wondered if Private Hunecke was among those repatriated. I sent a letter of inquiry to the Jefferson Barracks National Cemetery and received a prompt and thorough email reply from Mr. David Rogers, Administrative Officer. My email exchange with Mr. Rogers provided insight into the dedicated people who serve the families of deceased veterans at national cemeteries throughout the country. I received his email in late morning on the Saturday of Memorial Day weekend 2012. In my reply I commented on the fact that he was working on a holiday weekend. He replied:

"This is our biggest weekend of the year, as you can well imagine. We will have many thousands of visitors come to the cemetery over the next few days, as well as numerous ceremonies throughout the weekend. It is our honor to care for these veterans and their families."

Mr. Rogers reported that Private Hunecke was indeed one of those repatriated and was interred on July 9, 1949. His grave, marked with a simple white headstone, is less than 15 miles from the house on Tower Grove Place he left in 1943 to answer his country's call.

I Would Have Gone To My Grave Not Knowing Where My Brother Was Buried

FROM: Private Bryce Crosby; Ft. Polk, La.; July 20, 1943; marked as "No. 1" of multiple cards

TO: His wife Margie in Flint, Mich.

MESSAGE: *"Hello my sweetheart. Oh I love you my darling. I am in the service club dear. It is early forenoon, and I just came from the dentist a little while ago. He didn't pull my teeth but I have to go back at one o'clock and get them pulled. Read on next post card. Oh I love you. Your loving husband, Bryce."*

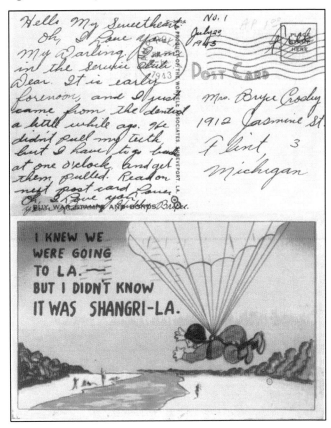

At age 86, Vanda Mitchell still has her natural hair color, still lives independently, and still remembers that terrible day in 1945 when she learned her brother, Private Bryce Eldon Crosby, had been killed in the war.

It was Sunday, May 6, 1945, and Vanda was a senior at Grand Blanc High School near Flint, Mich. She was at a friend's house near her family's farm, practicing for a song she and the friend were to sing at church that evening. When the phone sounded the "party line" ring signaling a call for Vanda's family, she picked up the phone and overheard her parents getting the word that Bryce was dead. His wife, as next of kin, had received the official notification and was calling to inform his parents.

While Vanda was at school the next day, Monday, May 7, the news came that Germany had surrendered. "Everybody else at school was celebrating, and I was crying," Vanda recalls.

I learned the story of Bryce Crosby and met his sister Vanda through a postcard he wrote July 20, 1943 from Camp Polk, La., to his wife, Margie, at their home in Flint. The card began, "Hello my

Bryce Crosby's 1940 high school graduation portrait and an undated snapshot at an Army base during the war.

sweetheart." The opening and closing sentences were, "Oh, I love you." He told her he had been to the dentist that morning and was going back in the afternoon to have some teeth pulled. He signed it, "Your loving hubby, Bryce."

Like many WWII postcards, this one featured a cartoon of military life. It showed a paratrooper gliding down toward a beach full of women in swimsuits. In a play on the postal abbreviation for Louisiana, it said, "I knew we were going to La. But I didn't know it was Shangri-La."

The message was labeled as the first of multiple cards and said he would continue the message on the next card. I bought the card on eBay in 2012, but never found the second card.

It took me a couple of months of searching to find Bryce's family. There was no evidence he had children, so I started looking for siblings or his widow. I learned from the 1930 census that he was born in 1922, the eldest of three children of William and Charlotte Crosby. His siblings were a brother, Robert, and sister, Vanda.

From the Genesee County Clerk's web site I learned Bryce married Margie May Palmer on June 20, 1942. She remarried in 1953, eight years after his death, and I could find no further record of her. That left the siblings as my only chance of finding his family.

Bryce's brother Robert died in 2002. I was unable to locate his children, but the list of survivors in his obituary

AMERICAN BATTLE MONUMENTS COMMISSION

THE WORLD WAR II HONOR ROLL

Bryce E. Crosby

Private First Class, U.S. Army

Service # 36531284

414th Infantry Regiment, 104th Infantry Division

Entered the Service from: Michigan
Died: 13-Apr-45
Buried at: Plot G Row 5 Grave 20
Netherlands American Cemetery
Margraten, Netherlands

Awards: Purple Heart

Bryce Crosby's burial site is recorded on the web site of the American Battle Monuments Commission.

named a sister, Vanda Mitchell. I found an address for a person by that name in Flint on Switchboard.com and sent her a letter.

About a week later Vanda called me, surprised that I had tracked her down. She said, "I'm the last one left in the family. I don't know how much longer the good Lord will keep me here, but I'd like to have the postcard and pass it on to my cousins."

Vanda told me her brother was a nice, quiet man who didn't drink or use profanity. She spoke of what a short a time he had with his bride before shipping out with the Army. She said that after the war, Bryce's widow contacted one of his Army buddies, and he told her the circumstances of Bryce's death.

Vanda Mitchell with photos of her brother, Bryce Eldon Crosby (right) who was killed in World War II; and her son, Bryce Eldon Ankney, who served in Vietnam.

Bryce Crosby was killed by an enemy bullet near the town of Nordhausen, Germany, on April 13, 1945, as he walked alongside a tank, his Browning Automatic Rifle at the ready. It was one day after President Franklin D. Roosevelt died. While news of Roosevelt's death was almost instantly flashed around the country, it was three weeks before word reached the Crosby family that Bryce was dead.

Bryce and Margie were married on June 20, 1942 and had only a few months of married life together before he was called to the Army. His memorial service was held at the same downtown Flint church where he and Margie were married less than three years earlier.

I first corresponded with Vanda and talked with her on the phone in April 2012. That September, after my wife Becky and I retired and moved to Michigan, we visited her one Sunday afternoon at her apartment not too many miles from the family farm where she and Bryce grew up. She greeted us warmly, invited us in, and sat down in her favorite chair. On the wall behind her was a tapestry with the phrase "God Bless America" and two framed photographs of men in uniform. One is her brother, and the other is her son, Bryce Eldon Ankney, who carries his uncle's name and has two Purple Hearts from his service in Vietnam.

When I think of Bryce Crosby I think of what might have been had he returned safely to Flint. The Flint economy may be struggling these days, but it was a boomtown in the post-war years. Before the war Bryce Crosby worked at an AC Spark Plug plant. Had he lived he would probably have returned to that job and raised a family during the heyday of the auto industry. He would have made a good income, lived in a solid middle-class neighborhood, traded for a new Buick every few years, and maybe even owned a cabin "up north" as Michiganders call it.

Instead he had only a few fleeting months with his bride, shipped off to Europe, was in combat for seven straight months, and died in battle. In addition to seeing the horror of war on a daily basis, he might also have witnessed an even greater horror the day before he died. Bryce was a member of the 104th Infantry, which liberated the Nazi's Dora-Nordhausen slave labor camp on April 12, 1945. On May 5, 1945, three weeks after Bryce was killed, the 104th saw its last combat. The unit departed Europe to return home on June 27, 1945.

Bryce is buried in the Netherlands American Cemetery in Margraten, Netherlands. A photo of his grave marker is posted on Findagrave. When I sent Vanda her brother's postcard I included a photo of his marker pulled from the internet. She wrote back thanking me for the card and added that were it not for my contact with her, "I would have gone to my grave not knowing where my brother was buried." That photo of the simple white cross marking Bryce Crosby's grave in the Netherlands now hangs on her apartment wall.

Bryce Crosby's grave marker in the Netherlands.

Honoring the Memory of the Hoffer Brothers

FROM: Private Woodrow Hoffer, Camp Forrest, Tenn.; June 22, 1942

TO: A cousin, Maxine Corne, in his hometown of Monroe, Mich.

MESSAGE: *"I got your letter some time ago. But this is the first time I could write. I hope that things are OK. Mother wrote a card from Ohio. I don't know when I get a pass now. We have our 8 weeks in now. Five weeks yet to go then things be easy to what they are now.. Your old man still go to school yet? My leg isn't so hot but doctor said he couldn't help any as for I am fit to march."*

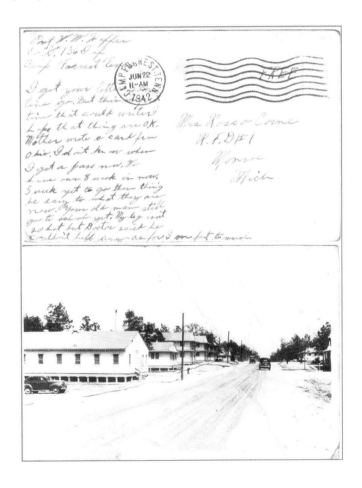

Private Woodrow Wilson Hoffer wrote a postcard in 1942 from an Army post in Tennessee to a relative back home in Monroe, Mich. Seventy years later that postcard led me to the story of two brothers who died in combat, a four-star mother who steadfastly endured unimaginable sorrow, two men who carry the names of heroic uncles they never knew, and a community that never forgets its veterans.

Woodrow Hoffer's postcard to his cousin, Maxine Corne, is dated June 22, 1942. It's typical of cards written by soldiers during boot camp. He mentioned receiving a letter from his mother, inquired about Maxine's "old man," and closed with, "My leg isn't so hot but the doctor says he couldn't help any as I am fit to march." I bought the card on eBay from a seller in New Jersey and started hunting for Woodrow. Finding his trail was easy, as there was only one Woodrow Hoffer in the National Archives' database of World War II enlistments.

No sooner did I find his enlistment record than I discovered he was killed in action on Morotai Island in the Pacific Dec. 31, 1944. That information led me to a web site honoring "Fallen Heroes of Monroe County." Featured at the top of the page was Monroe County's most famous military son, General George Custer.

Scrolling down I found Woodrow's photo. It was like thousands of other photos taken of soldiers during boot camp, a head-and-shoulders shot of a smiling young man in uniform, cap tilted jauntily to one side.

Then I noticed the photo next to Woodrow's. It was a younger man named Staff Sergeant Marion Edward Hoffer, killed in action in Europe Feb. 27, 1945, just 58 days after Woodrow's death. I wondered if they were brothers.

The answer came readily enough. Through Google and a stroke of luck with a newspaper article I soon confirmed that Woodrow and Marion Hoffer were indeed brothers. I also found one of their relatives. On Memorial Day 2009, the Monroe chapter of Veterans of Foreign Wars held a ceremony honoring the 825 soldiers from Monroe who died in wars. The program was reported in the *Monroe News*, and near the bottom of the article I read:

"When the images of Marion and Woodrow Hoffer appeared, it became very personal for Norma Stahl of Monroe. They were her uncles, her father's brothers, and both were killed during World War II. Mrs. Stahl appreciated the tribute.

Although Woodrow and Marion Hoffer are buried thousands of miles from their hometown of Monroe, Mich., their memory lives on at a monument in Veterans' Park and on benches placed by their family in a local cemetery.

"'I loved it,'" she said. 'I never knew either of my uncles but my grandmother always told stories about them. We heard a lot of stories.'"

I located an address for Norma Stahl and wrote her a letter, enclosing a photocopy of Woodrow's postcard and offering to return it to the family. Within days I received an email from Norma, saying in part:

"Thank you so much for your correspondence about my uncles. What a surprise to hear my uncle's names mentioned in your letter. Thank you for brightening my day!"

I also received a phone call from Norma's brother Ed, the unofficial Hoffer family historian. From Norma's email and an hour-long phone call with Ed I learned about the Hoffer brothers, their legacy, and the amazing strength of their mother.

Woodrow Hoffer was born in 1912, and his brother Marion in 1922, sons of Bernice and Mary Hoffer. They had two other brothers, Bill and Melvin, and a sister, Almeda. At the time I contacted the family in March 2012 Almeda was the only surviving sibling, living in Vermont. Melvin died in a traffic accident in 1963, and Bill passed away in 2010 at age 84.

Neither Woodrow nor Marion had children. Woodrow was engaged to be married at the time of his death. His fiancé, who lived in Ohio, married after the war and the Hoffer family lost touch with her. Marion married in May 1944, less than a year before he died, but did not have children. Marion's widow remarried and had a family.

Although Woodrow and Marion did not have children, their names live on. Their brother Melvin named two sons "Woodrow" and "Edward Marion" in honor of his brothers. Woody and Ed still live in Monroe, as does their sister, Norma.

Woodrow and Marion are buried overseas in cemeteries maintained by the American Battle Monuments Commission. Woodrow's final resting place is at the Manila American Cemetery in the Philippines, and Marion's grave is in the Netherlands American Cemetery in Margraten, Netherlands. Norma relates that their sister, Almeda, visited Marion's grave in the Netherlands, and their sister-in-law, Betty, visited Woodrow's grave in the Philippines.

The American Battle Monuments Commission has an excellent web site with photos and information about the cemeteries managed by the Commission. From it I learned that Margraten includes 40 sets of brothers buried side-by-side. Another of my "postcard people," Bryce Crosby, is buried at Margraten. It is also the final resting place of PFC Walter Wetzel, who was posthumously awarded the Medal of Honor for throwing himself on enemy grenades to save his comrades. PFC Wetzel was from Roseville, Mich., about 50 miles from Monroe, home of the Hoffer family.

Although the Hoffer brothers are buried thousands of miles from home, and from each other, their memory lives on in their hometown.

Their names are inscribed together on a World War 2 memorial in Veterans' Park alongside the picturesque River Raisin, and they are honored together at Roselawn Memorial Park with matching granite benches placed by their brother Bill. The Monroe community also remembers the Hoffer brothers, and other sons lost in wars, with Memorial Day ceremonies.

Ed told me his grandmother often spoke of Woodrow and Marion, and the family has letters and other mementos of them. One such memento is a letter Marion's father wrote to him at Thanksgiving 1944. The letter came back as undeliverable. Shortly thereafter came the news that Marion was dead. The family also has Woodrow's last letter to his parents, written from New Guinea just eight days before he died.

Although Ed was born after his uncles died, he knows a lot about them. He says that while he was growing up in Monroe people would see the Hoffer name, recall Woodrow and Marion, and tell stories about them.

Like many places in Michigan, Monroe is an auto industry town. Woodrow worked at Auto Equipment Company and Marion at Monroe Steel Castings (known for Monroe shock absorbers). Ed recounted that Woodrow was also an entrepreneur. "He had a monopoly on newspaper stands in Monroe," Ed recalled.

Woodrow's obituary confirms he was a go-getter from an early age. It reported, "He attended the public schools, sold papers, and shined shoes for Nick Vivilakis." (Mr. Vivilakis was a Greek immigrant who ran a shoe repair shop in Monroe. Nick's son, Jimmie, was inducted in 1942 and returned home safely. The Vivilakis family later joined the post-war migration to California.) Ed says Woodrow was reportedly a good money manager and paid cash for a house that he left to his parents when he died.

Marion, according to the stories Ed heard, was a good dancer and "in tip top condition." Ed heard stories of how Marion "stuck up for" a boy who had a speech impediment when other children taunted him.

Becky and I had the privilege of visiting with Norma Stahl, niece of Woodrow and Marion, at her home in Monroe in October 2012. She and her husband, Larry, graciously gave up watching a Detroit Tigers

Killed

WOODROW W. HOFFER

PFC. Woodrow W. Hoffer, son of Mr. and Mrs. Bernice L. Hoffer of 467 Mulhollen drive, was killed in action on Morotai Island December 31, 1944. He had been overseas since August 1943.

Inducted April 10, 1942 he was sent from Fort Sheridan, Illinois, to Camp Forrest, Tennessee, and then Breckinridge, Kentucky, returning to Camp Forrest. In the early fall of 1942 he was transferred to Fort Lewis, Washington, and spent eight days with his parents that December. He was in California for desert training three months just before going to Hawaii in August, 1943. From Hawaii he went to New Guinea and it was from there a letter came dated last December 23 saying he was to be transferred and would write later.

He was born December 11, 1912 in Delphos, Ohio, and at the age of seven moved to Monroe with his parents. He attended the public schools, sold papers and shined shoes for Nick Vivilakis. He was employed at the Auto Equipment Company when he entered service.

He is survived by his parents; three brothers, Melvin of Southgate Heights, Sergeant Marion in Germany with the 9th Army and Private William of the AAF stationed at Big Springs, Texas; a sister, Mrs. A. J. Johnson of Essex, Connecticut; his grandmother, Mrs. Martha Derickson of Ida; three uncles, three aunts and two nephews. His fiancee, Miss Elsie Geething, lives at Grover Hills, Ohio.

Killed

MARION E. HOFFER

Staff Sergeant Marion E. Hoffer was killed in action February 27 in the European theater, according to word received by his parents and wife Friday. He was the son of Mr. and Mrs. Bernice Hoffer of 467 Mulhollen drive and husband of the former Doris Dahl, of 422 Harrison street. Sergeant Hoffer had recently been awarded the Bronze Star for heroic achievement in action in France. He was 22 years old, born October 10, 1922. He was inducted December 17, 1942, while employed at the Monroe Steel Castings. In May of 1944 he married Miss Dahl.

A brother PFC. Woodrow W. Hoffer, 32, was killed in December on Moratai Island. Another brother William, a private, is in training at the AAF base at Big Springs, Texas. Other survivors are a sister Mrs. A. I. Johnson of Essex, Connecticut, a brother, Melvin, at home and his grandmother, Mrs. Martha Derick of Ida.

Obituaries like these for the Hoffer brothers were all too common in hometown newspapers large and small during World War II.

playoff game to talk with me about her uncles. She shared family photos and showed me a book published by the local VFW that included a chapter about Woodrow and Marion. She and Larry took us to the Roselawn Cemetery to see the benches placed by their family in honor of Woodrow and Marion.

Woodrow and Marion are not the only World War II heroes in the Hoffer family. Their story is not complete without mention of their mother, Mary Derickson Hoffer.

The Courage Of A Four-Star Mother

Men who die in combat are remembered as heroes and honored with parades, monuments and ceremonies. Standing behind them are their mothers, living lives of quiet heroism and quiet desperation. In the Hoffer family of Monroe, Mich., that person was Mary Derickson Hoffer.

When Mrs. Hoffer observed Christmas in 1944 she had three sons in the service – Woodrow, Marion, and Bill. In the next seven weeks both Woodrow and Marion were killed in action. Her fourth son Melvin, who was living safely in Monroe, enlisted after learning of his brothers' deaths.

Ed Hoffer, nephew of Woodrow and Marion, speaks fondly of his grandmother and her strength: "She had two gold stars and two blue stars on her door. I can't fathom her sitting in that house, wondering every time a car turned around in the driveway if it was Western Union. It didn't hit home for me until I saw 'Saving Private Ryan.' How did she live day to day with that pressure?" (A blue star on the door denoted a son in the service, while a gold star meant a son had been killed in action.)

When I think of Mrs. Hoffer, looking out her window, wondering if that car in the driveway was the Western Union man, I recall the words written to a grieving mother by Abraham Lincoln in 1864: ". . . the solemn pride that must be yours to have laid so costly a sacrifice upon the altar of freedom." Lincoln's quote is inscribed on the National Memorial Cemetery of the Pacific in Honolulu and was used in the movie "Saving Private Ryan." (There is much debate over the origin of this quote; I leave that to others.)

Ed's sister, Norma Stahl, remembers their grandmother's strength despite having lost two sons and a nephew in the war, and a third son, Norma's father, in a traffic accident. Norma wrote:

"Grandma lived to be 100 and passed in 1992. Her beauty, strength, sense of humor, and kindness to others, after suffering so much loss, has always been such an inspiration to me."

My Own Personal Connection

As I was putting the finishing touches on this book, I just happened to find my own personal connection to a card from World War II and a soldier who was killed in action. This one was not a postcard; it was my mother's identification card from her job at an Army installation in 1943.

My mother, Annie Lee Richardson Schlatter, grew up in Centreville, a small town in southwest Mississippi. During the war, Centreville was home to Camp Van Dorn, one of many Army training camps hastily built throughout the country.

As a teenager she kept the books at her father's grocery store. After graduating from Centreville High School her bookkeeping experience helped her get a job in the payroll department of a construction company building the camp hospital. She left the job after marrying my father in November 1943 and moved to St. Louis, where he was stationed at Jefferson Barracks.

After my mother died in 2007, one of the mementos we found in her files was her identification card from Camp Van Dorn. I kept the card, but as I was sorting things out in preparation for retiring in the summer of 2012 my brother and I decided to donate it to the Camp Van Dorn Museum in Centreville.

As I was putting the card in the envelope to mail it to the museum I noticed a detail I had

When my mother worked at Camp Van Dorn in Mississippi during the war, her identification card was signed by the camp's Provost Marshall, Lt. Lorenzo D. Suggs, Jr.

previously overlooked. The card was signed by the Provost Marshall, Lt. Lorenzo D. Suggs, Jr. Having just spent several months researching World War II records in the course of writing this book, I decided to see what I could find about Lt. Suggs.

I learned that Lt. Suggs died January 13, 1945, from wounds suffered during the Battle of the Bulge. He was with the 90th Infantry Division, one of the units that trained at Camp Van Dorn. A native of South Carolina, Lt. Suggs was a graduate of Clemson University where he was on the boxing and track teams. He is buried in Horry County, South Carolina, not far from my daughter's home in Murrells Inlet.

Lt. Lorenzo D. Suggs, Jr. died of wounds inflicted at the Battle of the Bulge.

I was able to locate his son, Lorenzo D. Suggs, III, a retired Postmaster living in Santee, S.C., and send him a copy of the card containing his father's signature. As it happens, Mr. Suggs and I share an interest in golf, and we plan an outing the next time I visit South Carolina. He sent me the following information about his father:

"My mother spoke of Dad's assignment in Mississippi and the fine people they met while stationed there. Dad was later shipped overseas because so many were being killed and they needed more officers. As your research shows, Dad was killed in action in the Battle of the Bulge. Not to bore you but my father came from a rural farming family of nine children, five girls and four boys, dad being the baby boy. I have a picture of him standing by Herbert Hoover, President of the United States, and along with the Secretary of Agriculture in front of the White House. Dad was the corn growing champion of 1930 at 122 bushels per acre according to the photo I have."

In subsequent correspondence Mr. Suggs told me he, his mother, and his younger brother lived in Centreville while his dad was stationed at Camp Van Dorn. He was about three years old at the time. Mr. Suggs said his father was Methodist and his mother was Baptist, and they were "church going" people. Centreville is a tiny town, and I wonder if my mother might have run into the Suggs family. Her family was in the pews at Centreville Baptist Church every time the door was open. I wonder if Lt. Suggs' wife attended the same services as my mother's family. Did Mrs. Suggs shop at my grandfather's grocery store? Did my mother meet Lt. Suggs when he signed her ID card? I'll never know, but it seems likely that she and the Suggs family crossed paths at some time or the other.

Synchronicity

One of my favorite movies is "Grand Canyon," starring Kevin Kline, Danny Glover, Mary McDonnell, and Steve Martin (in one of his non-comedy roles). When the movie came out in 1991, my friend Lois Martin recommended it. I asked her the usual question ("What's it about?"), and she cryptically replied, "Synchronicity." That was a new word for me.

The movie tells the story of characters from very different walks of life who would ordinarily never meet, but they become connected in meaningful ways through a series of apparently unrelated events. Each character gains something from the others. After seeing the movie I began to understand what Lois meant by "synchronicity." There are many definitions of that word. To me, it's the concept that seemingly random things sometimes happen for a reason.

It was more than just chance that I bought those first postcards and started researching them. Why did postcards from Livermore Falls show up in a junk store in Colorado? Why did a guy like me who never had the slightest interest in postcards buy them? Why did I start trying to find the writers or their family? I believe it was synchronicity, for without those random events the stories of these American heroes would have remained untold.

When I read Tom Brokaw's landmark book, "The Greatest Generation," I was struck by his accounts of the quiet courage of the men and women who fought in World War II and the exemplary lives they led after the war. That feeling comes back to me when I reflect on my "postcard people."

These men and women did extraordinary things. They and their families endured hardship and loss. Some, like Sid Campbell at Dachau, witnessed unspeakable horror. Some didn't come home. All are heroes in one way or another.

I hope this book, in some small way, does justice to their memory.

Reference List of Postcards

The following table shows each postcard or set of cards from this book, who wrote them, and where they ended up.

THE WRITER	THE POSTCARD	THE SEARCH
Private Cecilia Aragon (later Cecilia Guzman)	From Camp Lejune, N.C., to a former teacher in Santa Fe, N.M., 1942.	Cecilia has passed away. Card returned to her daughter in Colorado Springs, Colo.
Gus Luschenat, U.S. Navy	From Naval Training Center, Sampson, N.Y.; anniversary greeting to his wife Josephine in Waterbury, Conn., Aug. 8, 1944	Gus passed away in 1990. Card was lost in a flood in 1955, reappeared on eBay in 2012, returned to Josephine in Florida.
Sgt. August Mommens	From Columbus, Miss. to his little sister, Vernabelle, in Nebraska, November 1943	Sgt. Mommens became a minister. He passed away in 2005. Vernabelle is a great-grandmother at age 80-plus. Card returned to the family.
PFC Clark McWilliams	Mailed from Ft. Lewis, Wash., Dec. 8, 1943, to the family of his future wife.	Card returned to Mr. McWilliams a few weeks before his death in April 2012.
PFC Fred Hegler	Mailed from Wichita Falls, Tex., to his parents in Pueblo, Colo., 1945.	Mr. Hegler still lives in Pueblo. Card returned to him.
Private Sid Campbell and Private David Henson	One card from each man to a girl named Sue, a friend of Sid back home in Louisiana, 1943.	David passed away in 2008. Card returned to his daughter. Sid and David remained friends long after the war. Sid's card was returned to him in March 2012; he passed away in September.
Lt. George Moses	V-Mail letter written from North Africa to Gary Rogness, newborn son of Lt. Don Rogness, when he was born in 1943. Lt. Moses was friends with the baby's father, Lt. Don Rogness.	Lt. Moses and Lt. Rogness have both passed away. Letter was returned to Gary Rogness, who was the subject of the birthday greeting. He is a retired Los Angeles police officer.
PFC William Halfen	Postcard to his uncle in Delaware, 1944.	Mr. Halfen passed away in 2005. Unbeknownst to him, this card sat in an antique store near his home for two decades before being returned to his son in Baltimore.
PFC Bob Carrucci	One card each to his wife and his co-workers at a construction company back home in Brooklyn, 1945.	Bob and his wife have both passed away with no known survivors. They left major bequests to a university and a YMCA. Unable to find family members to return the card.

...ER	THE POSTCARD	THE SEARCH
..., girlfriend ...Staff Sgt. ...on.	Three cards from New York City to Sgt. Anderson at Camp Livingston, La., 1942.	Howard and Veronica were married for more than 60 years and are buried together in California. Unable to find relatives to return the cards.
...ussell Liddle and ...etty	Postcard written on their honeymoon from Ocean Grove, N.J. to his brother and wife back home in Massachusetts, 1942.	Sgt. Liddle and his wife Betty have passed away. Card returned to his son.
...ier named Harold (last ...e not used because could ...locate family)	Highly sentimental card written to his mother in Wisconsin, 1942.	Harold died in 1955. Unable to find any family members.
...ajor S. Howard Cohan ...Army dentist)	Postcard from Camp Edwards, Mass. to his daughter, Joanne, Oct. 29, 1942	Dr. Cohan and Joann have passed away. Card returned to her son in California.
Francis Folsom Clifton Eames Raymond Merrill	These three soldiers, all from Maine, sent a total of seven postcards to a mother and daughter in Livermore Falls, Maine. The recipients were relatives or neighbors of the soldiers.	Cards somehow ended up in a antique store in Colorado. All three men have passed away. Cards were returned to daughters of Eames and Folsom. Unable to find relatives of Raymond Merrill.
Captain David Morton	Card sent from an Air Corps base in Tennessee to his sister in Jessups, Md., 1942.	Captain Morton became a pilot and was killed when his plane went down during Battle of the Bulge. His sister, who became an Army nurse, has passed away. Card returned to a relative in Montana.
Private Adolph Hunecke	Card to friends back home in St. Louis, 1943.	Private Hunecke was killed in action in Italy in 1944 and is buried in St. Louis. Card returned to his nephew.
Private Bryce Crosby	Card from Camp Polk, La., to his wife back home in Flint, Mich., 1943.	Private Crosby was killed in action in Europe and is buried in the Netherlands. His wife remarried and has passed away. Card returned to his sister. She never knew where her brother was buried until being contacted about this postcard.
Private Woodrow Hoffer	Card from Camp Forrest, Tenn., to a cousin in his hometown of Monroe, Mich., 1943.	Private Hoffer was killed in action in late 1944, and his brother, Staff Sgt. Marion Hoffer, was killed in action seven weeks later. Two nephews bear their names. Card returned to the family.